This book is dedicated to my three favorite M's: Marinette, Marielle, and Mitchell.

Developing Android on Android

Automate Your Device with Scripts and Tasks

Mike Riley

The Pragmatic Bookshelf

Dallas, Texas • Raleigh, North Carolina

Many of the designations used by manufacturers and sellers to distinguish their products are claimed as trademarks. Where those designations appear in this book, and The Pragmatic Programmers, LLC was aware of a trademark claim, the designations have been printed in initial capital letters or in all capitals. The Pragmatic Starter Kit, The Pragmatic Programmer, Pragmatic Programming, Pragmatic Bookshelf, PragProg and the linking *g* device are trademarks of The Pragmatic Programmers, LLC.

Every precaution was taken in the preparation of this book. However, the publisher assumes no responsibility for errors or omissions, or for damages that may result from the use of information (including program listings) contained herein.

Our Pragmatic courses, workshops, and other products can help you and your team create better software and have more fun. For more information, as well as the latest Pragmatic titles, please visit us at *http://pragprog.com.*

The Android robot is reproduced or modified from work created and shared by Google and used according to terms described in the Creative Commons 3.0 Attribution License.

The team that produced this book includes:

Jacquelyn Carter (editor)
Potomac Indexing, LLC (indexer)
Molly McBeath (copyeditor)
David J Kelly (typesetter)
Janet Furlow (producer)
Juliet Benda (rights)
Ellie Callahan (support)

Printed in the United States of America.
ISBN-13: 978-1-937785-54-3
Printed on acid-free paper.
Book version: P1.0—November 2013

Contents

Part IV — Appendixes

Acknowledgments

This is my second book for Pragmatic Bookshelf, and it has been a pleasure to once again work with my dedicated and insightful development editor, Jackie Carter. If you can follow along with the projects without any problem, you have Jackie to thank. Her editorial skills and professional project management were crucial in keeping the book flowing smoothly and on schedule.

I would also like to thank all the wonderful technical editors and beta reader participants who shared valuable feedback, caught typos and other errors, and generally offered excellent suggestions on improving the quality of the book. In particular, I would like to thank Mike Bengtson for his awesome ingenuity, Corey Butler for his progressive technical edge, Ed Burnette for his pragmatic expertise, John Cairns for his eagle-eye criticality, and Glen Ferrel for his proofreading expertise and infectious enthusiasm. I also want to give a big shout-out to Dr. James Withers and Simon Wood (two of the geniuses behind the awesome SwiftKey Android soft keyboard replacement program) for their eagle-eye analysis of the book's content. And a special thank-you goes to Jan Debiec and Cristina Zamora for their vigilant review of the material, active participation in the beta, and unending encouragement for my work. I am so blessed and humbled to be surrounded by such technically minded people as gifted, kind, and supportive as you.

No amount of thanks can match the sacrifice my family made to give me the time to devote to another book. I promise to take a break from book writing for a while so I can make up for lost time with you.

Lastly, a big high-five to publishers Andy Hunt and Dave Thomas for once again entrusting me to deliver a book worthy of the Pragmatic Bookshelf imprint. Thank you for giving me such a wonderfully rewarding opportunity to do so.

Introduction

In this book, we're going on a journey of discovery. We're going to discover how amazing the Android OS is and how it is transforming the way people communicate. We're also going to learn how to leave our legacy desktop PCs behind, even for native Android application development needs.

The idea for this book was the result of a conversation I had with Pragmatic Bookshelf publisher Dave Thomas. He had just acquired a Galaxy S3 Android phone and wanted to know what kind of cool things he could do with it. Since I have been an Android user since the release of the first commercial Android phone, the G1, I had a few suggestions on where to start. As he became more enthusiastic about the broad possibilities of customization and personalization that the Android platform has to offer, a new book on the subject started to crystallize.

The objectives of this book are simple. You will learn about how to apply and codify your mobile automation needs in an Android program. Using both scripting and native application development approaches, we will build several programs that not only teach you how to quickly automate your mobile lifestyle but also give you the skills to extend these programs beyond their tutorial roots.

Why Android? Why Now?

The Android OS is several years old, and its design principles (a modern, true multitasking mobile OS with built-in memory, permissions management, and so on) have been the same since its inception. So why is this book relevant now compared to five years ago, when Android was first introduced?

Obviously, the platform has matured considerably in that time. It has also greatly benefited from its open source approach by fostering significantly faster innovation compared to closed, proprietary operating systems. Take a look at a first-generation iPhone compared to the iPhone 5. While the hardware has vastly improved, the primary user interface is nearly identical. Consider the differences between Android 1.0 running on a G1 phone and Android 4.2 running on a Nexus 4. The differences are striking. The user interface, hardware support, design aesthetics, and everything but the original design principles have rapidly evolved for the better. One benefit from this co-evolution of hardware and software is that you can do things on a modern Android device that was the stuff of fiction five years ago. To think that on your Android device you can now do computing on a scale that was the exclusive domain of desktop PCs for the last thirty years is awe-inspiring.

This evolutionary path is also manifested in Android application development tools. Once clunky and incomplete, the Android SDK and Eclipse plug-ins are finally capable of stable, team-based, test-driven development. While the user interface construction toolkit could still use more polish, every other aspect of the typical Android development and emulation on a desktop PC is polished and professional.

One of the most exciting aspects of Android programming, testing, and deployment is that its application development life cycle can now be done directly on the Android device. This is a big deal. When compared to other mobile operating systems that require an expensive PC outfitted with a decent processor and plenty of RAM to run the target emulator, the projects discussed in this book require only your Android device. When you code and run applications on the same device, it greatly accelerates the development process, just as it did during the desktop PC era.

Let's also not forget that, like a desktop computer, Android's home screen can be highly customized and extended via custom wallpapers, animations, icons, folder actions, transition animations, and much more. This degree of personalization allows you to make your Android device fit your aesthetic values, daily workflow, and communication and notification preferences, not the other way around. Third-party extensions and widgets also help push the envelope of what is possible, further contributing to Android's success and dominant market position.

Who This Book Is For

This book is for anyone who is interested in doing much more with an Android device than downloading and using apps from the Google Play store. If you love your Android phone or tablet and you love to tinker with technology, this is the perfect book for you. And while prior programming experience is not required, it will be helpful to understand some of the scripts that we will create in the chapters ahead.

Requirements

This is a book about Android, so it should come as no surprise that a must-have requirement is an Android phone or tablet running Android OS 4.2 (known by its friendly code name Jelly Bean) or newer. The screenshots used throughout this book were taken on a Galaxy Nexus phone and Nexus 7 tablet.

In addition to the Android phone or tablet, you should have an active account on the Google Play store, since a good portion of the software used in this book is exclusively distributed via the Google Play service.

Lastly, while it's not required, I strongly recommend you obtain a quality Bluetooth keyboard known to be compatible with the Android OS. I have yet to use a Bluetooth keyboard that could not be paired with Android, but keyboards designed specifically with Android in mind are optimal since they often have special keys associated with functions such as play/pause music, volume control, toggle between applications, lock the screen, and so on. My current favorite mobile Bluetooth keyboard is the Logitech Tablet Keyboard for Win8/RT and Android, shown in the following figure.[1] It is a full-size keyboard and thus larger than other mobile Bluetooth keyboards that have a smaller footprint or fold in half for greater portability. Plus, Logitech's full-size keyboard combined with the protective cover doubles as a phone or tablet stand.

Figure 1—The Logitech Tablet Keyboard for Win8/RT and Android

---

1. http://www.logitech.com/en-us/tablet-accessories/android/tablet-keyboard-android-win8-rt

While you are understandably not going to be able to use this keyboard in a cramped moving vehicle such as a bus or train, it works perfectly fine sitting on an airplane fold-down seat tray or desk. And since I'm usually bringing along a backpack during my commutes, the Logitech keyboard adds practically no additional weight or bulk to the bag. Besides, you will find that the keyboard is a sanity saver when editing code or documents on the Android device.

So, that's it—a phone or tablet, an active Google Play account, and maybe an Android-compatible Bluetooth keyboard. For folks like me who have been around since the dawn of the personal computer era, it is simply amazing to think how far we have come in the past forty years and how much further we'll go in the next forty years.

Jailbreaking and Rooting

Unlike traditional desktop operating systems, mobile OSs like Android and iOS are locked down in such a way so that the system-level files cannot be tampered with by ordinary users. This keeps the device more secure by preventing malicious applications from modifying system files without the user's knowledge. Similarly, it prevents the user from altering these files.

Jailbreaking is a term used in the mobile device market to mean a procedure that allows users to bypass the normal operating system–level restrictions, typically to gain root-level access (*rooting* the device). Once root access is obtained, the user or application has full read-write access to all aspects of the operating system files. This allows modification of the device's behavior in ways that weren't originally intended by the OS developer.

While Android OS tinkerers can benefit from rooting a device by understanding the internal workings of the OS better, average users could be putting the contents and operation of their phones' security at risk if they are untrained in the various aspects of mobile OS security best practices. In the early days of Android, when many features were immature or missing, jailbreaking and rooting were more attractive, since doing so provided power users with a degree of customization that matched their needs. These custom modifications could range from modifying system-level virtual private network (VPN) software stacks to changing the look and feel of the home screen.

Android today is a much more mature operating system, so many of these limitations have a viable and more secure alternative. The projects in this book do not require jailbreaking or rooting your device. Unless you are a security researcher or a technology tinkerer who likes to crack things open to see how they work, there is no overwhelming reason for average users to consider jailbreaking and rooting their Android devices.

What's in This Book

Now that we have packed our bags for the journey, let's look at the road map we'll use to progress along the trail.

In the first part of the book, we will look at the variety of options we have to customize our Android experience. The home screen, lock screen, widgets, backgrounds, icons, and touch behaviors can all be personalized to your liking. Unlike some mobile operating systems that enforce a structured, inflexible design aesthetic, Android offers desktop-like customization in a mobile package. We will dive into specific examples for home screen renovation. We will also take a look at extending our Android experience by calling upon a variety of Android's hardware capabilities, such as using the headphone jack to transform our Android applications into better, more convenient, and information-rich wearable-computing user experiences.

In Part II, we will dip our toe in the automation waters by taking a look at a very powerful application called Tasker. We will use Tasker to automate several personal workflow needs and get introduced to some basic conditional programming and control flow while we're at it. We will also delve further into the programming landscape with the introduction of Scripting Layer for Android (SL4A). SL4A will allow us to write scripts in Python, Ruby, and other popular interpreted languages that will execute on Android and give us access to most of the system-level calls exposed by the Android SDK. We will conclude the Explore section of the book by actually programming Android using the native SDK. But instead of using a personal computer loaded with the Android SDK, emulator, and related development tools, we will write, compile, test, and deploy these native applications entirely on our Android phone or tablet.

In Part III of the book, we will apply what we learned in the first two parts by first creating a custom Android widget entirely on the device—no PC required. The final set of projects in the book will wrap these scripting and automation technologies in friendly user interfaces. These projects will show the versatility and automation opportunities that Android has to offer. The book also includes appendixes that review a variety of programming tools that run on the Android platform, as well as offer additional web resources to further your own project ideas.

By the end of the book, you should be well prepared to continue the journey on your own to create an Android experience that perfectly complements your information-interaction lifestyle.

Online Help

Many websites are devoted to the dissemination of Android news, reviews, hacking, modding, and programming. Check out Appendix 1, *Android Programming Tools*, on page 187, for a list of some of my favorites. It should go without saying that for Android development, Google's http://developer.android.com website offers the official word on Android application development. This isn't just a repository of bland technical documentation but a wealth of useful and well-written articles, tutorials, and tech notes from the folks responsible for various portions of the operating system. It's a resource that any serious Android developer should have permanently bookmarked.

There are a number of footnotes in the book featuring web links to more online resources. I also encourage you to post specific questions or comments about the ideas presented in the book at the book's web forum. Should you happen to spot an error, feel free to mention it on the book's website errata page. You're also welcome to contact me directly via my mike@mikeriley.com email address or follow me on Twitter @mriley. I look forward to hearing from you!

With that, we're ready to take a look at all the things we can customize in a nonrooted device running the stock Android 4.2 or newer operating system.

Mike Riley
mike@mikeriley.com
November 2013

Part I

Customize

CHAPTER 1

Getting Started

Today's smartphones are amazing devices. They are such powerful and capable computing devices that they have even replaced traditional desktop personal computers for some people. And like traditional desktops, one of the most exciting aspects of the Android platform, especially when compared to other mobile operating systems, is its ability to be highly customized. This customization goes beyond just wallpaper and icon replacements. You can use Android to create custom tasks, scripts, workflows, and behaviors that can't be done easily on most other mobile platforms.

In this book we're going to go beyond simply locating and installing commercial Android applications that provide generic functionality to fulfill your needs. But before we can start crafting scripts and applications that do what generic Android applications cannot, we need to evaluate key features of what an Android device has to offer. Then we can determine what to look for in the Google Play market. If we can't find what we're looking for, we can build it ourselves.

In this chapter, we will take a look at some of these key aspects before decking out your phone or tablet with themes, widgets, and applications that might not optimally suit your mobile lifestyle needs.

1.1 Analyzing Your Mobile Lifestyle

Before you can begin building a solution, you need to determine the problem to be solved. Even though today's high-end smartphones are more powerful than desktop computers were only a few years ago, this power is often not fully harnessed by users until they learn how to leverage all facets of the device. To do that, compare how you use your smartphone today with how you would like to use it in the future.

If your Android device is a phone, do you use it primarily for voice calls or texting? If you use an Android tablet, is it used mostly for reading ebooks or for surfing the Web? Deciding where you spend the most time with your device will help narrow down what functionality can be enhanced to improve your efficiency and satisfaction with the Android OS.

Think about how much time you spend with an application. Is it because it is so helpful that you can't imagine life without it? Or is it because the application is so cumbersome and nonintuitive that it sucks up a substantial amount of time while you're fighting the interface? Do you find yourself running the same type of task over and over again?

If you had the chance to re-create your most frequently used applications, what would you change about them? Do you have special needs that are not addressed in these apps?

Here is a personal example. I am bound by train schedules for my commute into work. As such, an important feature that I needed from my Android phone was a way for me to know the current time without having to dig into my pocket for my phone and fumble with the security unlock code. Just imagine how cumbersome that would be wearing thick gloves on a subzero Chicago winter morning. Since I was already wearing earbuds to actively listen to tech podcasts during my commute, hearing the time spoken was a much more advantageous solution than the visual clock display.

At first, I wrote a simple talking clock app using the Android SDK but found it to be inflexible when it came to making tweaks to the routines. If I discovered a bug or came up with an idea to extend the program's functionality, I had to wait until I got home to fire up my computer, run Eclipse, spin up an Android emulator, load the project, make changes to the codebase, go through a test/debug cycle in the emulator, and then push the compiled .apk file to my Android phone via the Android Debug Bridge (ADB). All that work for a few minor tweaks! Needless to say, there had to be a better way. Hence, the journey I'll take you through in this book mirrors my own iterations that best suited my mobile lifestyle needs.

If you're like me and you live in the post-PC era by deprecating your desktop or laptop computer for a phone or tablet alternative most of the time, your mobile lifestyle is all-encompassing. My phone is always by my side during my waking hours and on my nightstand when I sleep. Likewise, my tablet is with me during my commutes and anytime I'm driving somewhere where I will be away from home longer than an hour. Just as noteworthy to-dos pop into my head while on the go, ideas for enhancements to existing Android apps I have written have to be captured at that moment before they are lost into the ether of the day's demands.

Having the flexibility to make these changes on the fly has been about as game-changing for me as when I bought my first home computer in the 1980s (an Atari 400 with its craptaculous membrane keyboard) and then could write my own apps without having to wait for computer lab time at school. That freedom and flexibility changed my life back then, and as the Android platform matures with the ability to develop apps on the device rather than a hulking piece of hardware, that life-changing experience is resurfacing.

To put yourself in a mobile lifestyle frame of mind, here are some questions to ponder when considering how you use your Android device for your own customization opportunities:

- What hours of the day do you use your phone or tablet? If you respond "All the time," what are the time ranges that you use the device the most?

- What applications do you spend the most time using? If you're not sure, Android's Data Usage and Running apps (shown in the following figures) are accessible via the Android Settings application.

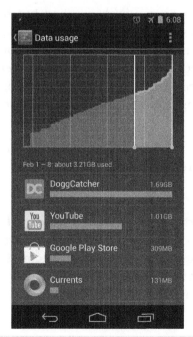

Figure 2—An example of Android's data usage

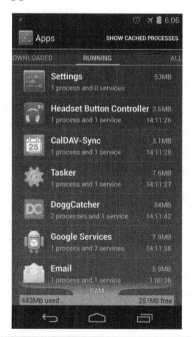

Figure 3—A list of currently running applications

While not a true reflection of time spent with each application, these two measurements can help you to a certain degree by showing you which programs consume the most bandwidth and power. These data collections can help you become more aware of which applications are frequently running (whether you're aware of them doing so in the background or not).

• What repetitive tasks do you perform with your device that would save time if you could automate these efforts? For example, I used to make an effort to turn on my phone every morning, turn on the WiFi radio, launch my podcast application (I'm currently a fan of the DoggCatcher Podcast Player[1]), and wait for the application to download whatever podcasts were available. When done, I would then turn off the WiFi radio to conserve battery. If I forgot or ran out of time, I wouldn't have any new podcasts to listen to on the way to work. By the way, I no longer do this manual process since I've scripted the entire procedure to kick off thirty minutes before I wake up. I've also created automated tasks to grab the latest news and weather to read to me after the clock alarm awakens me. We'll explore how to write your own scripts and tasks later in the book.

• What dream applications or widgets do you wish you had but haven't seen in the Google Play store? Be as specific as possible. Do you want an application that will wake you up, turn on the lights, and start brewing a pot of coffee at the same time? After reading this book and another book I wrote called *Programming Your Home [Ril12]*, also published by Pragmatic Bookshelf, you will have the knowledge necessary to bring an automation example like this to fruition.

With these thoughts in mind, let's take a closer look at some of the more interesting personal automation ideas we could build upon.

1.2 Mobile Personalization

After you have considered what opportunities for automation exist, start brainstorming how to make those ideas come to life. You will discover that the more you think about the improvements that customized automation can bring, the faster new program ideas will flow. Some of the automated scripts and applications that I have created on my Android devices include the following examples:

---

1. https://play.google.com/store/apps/details?id=com.snoggdoggler.android.applications.doggcatcher.v1_0

- Parse SMS alerts for keywords and react accordingly. If you're a system administrator, you could parse SMS messages for the phrase "Server down" and set off a klaxon-style alarm on your phone or tablet.

- Grab RSS news feeds and repackage them for your own personalized news broadcast. Set your Android device to connect to the Internet at specific times throughout the day to fetch RSS feeds, parse them, and convert the text to speech. Then have it read the news stories to you during your commute to and from work.

- Transmit Wake-On-LAN (WOL) packets in the middle of the night to computers on your LAN or home network. This will wake them up, run backups on their users' home directories, and send a backup report of success or failure to your Android device. Then let the computers go back to sleep.

- Have your Android phone automatically turn off all radios except mobile voice calls and set your display to night mode from the time you go to bed to the time you wake up in the morning. To help you fall asleep, have your phone play soothing music or sounds of nature (seashore, forest, meadow, rain shower, and so on) for twenty minutes, giving you enough time to peacefully fall asleep.

- Take a photo with your phone or tablet and have that image automatically cropped, filtered, resized, and posted to your online photo album or blog.

- Divert inbound phone calls based on caller ID information to voicemail or automatically forward the call to a secondary number (such as a Google Voice number that offers message transcription services) depending on time of day or level of personal importance.

Once you have a list of needs in mind, you can start to define what is necessary to bring these ideas to fruition. If someone hasn't already done the work for you and posted the results of their efforts online or in the Google Play store, you have a few more factors to consider before diving in and expending the time and effort needed to bring your ideas to life.

Consider Your Skill Level

If you consider yourself more of a power user than a programmer, you will find that most of the applications and tools mentioned in this book are easy and approachable. While some of the scripts require knowledge of the Python or Ruby language, it isn't essential that you know how to program in either. Tasks can be created with a minimum of programming knowledge, but it certainly helps if you have some coding skills and are willing to learn new things.

If you're already a programmer familiar with object-oriented languages like Java, picking up the necessary skills to develop Android applications is straightforward. Several books are available, and hundreds of text-based and video tutorials exist online to help get you started. As you will see later in this book, you can build applications that rival natively constructed commercial Android programs using these tools built for programmers and nonprogrammers alike.

Features vs. Time

When starting with an idea, I find it is best to begin with a prototype that can help crystallize how the application should behave. If I encounter constraints or roadblocks that simply cannot be overcome with the prototype, I make a note of these issues so I can evaluate whether those features are worth the effort to implement using more time-consuming native development approaches.

There are also times when writing automated tasks or scripts accomplishes enough of the intended objective that writing a native application is no longer necessary. This is particularly true if the script or workflow you are creating is targeted for your specific mobile lifestyle need. But what I have often discovered with my workflows is that as I show my creations to others, they excitedly ask whether they can have something similar. That's where this book comes in. As the classic Chinese proverb says, "Give a man a fish, and you feed him for a day. Teach a man to fish, and you feed him for a lifetime." Let's go fishing.

1.3 Next Steps

Keep the ideas presented in this chapter in mind as you read this book. As you learn how to make Android perform automated tasks, consider how these novel tasks can be expanded to make your life easier. The more you practice creativity, the more creative you will become.

In the next chapter, we will dive into our first layer of customization by modifying the look and feel of the Android home screen. With the help of a handful of utilities available from the Google Play store, we can transform the default Android user interface into a whole new experience.

CHAPTER 2

Personalizing Your Home Screen

For those old enough to remember the days of Windows 3.0, a key differentiator between that GUI-based operating system and the competing Apple Mac OS 7 was that Microsoft's offering allowed third-party shells to transform the look and feel of the Windows experience. As time went on and Microsoft's dominance was assured, this level of customization was practiced less frequently but could still be applied for those who preferred an alternative user interface.

Within the mobile space scenario, Google's Android has replaced Apple as the dominant operating system, in part because of the same openness to customizing the user experience. A variety of home-screen shells, better known as *launchers*, are available through the Google Play marketplace that can swap out default home-screen graphics, icons, and behaviors. And in contrast to Apple's iOS platform, Android allows the placement of onscreen mini-applications known as *widgets* to alter the stock Android UI. Pushing the envelope a bit further are what I call *floaters*. These are Android applications that run in a resizable desktop-like window that can multitask and hover on top of the home screen or other full-screen Android programs.

In this chapter, we will take a look at several home-screen customization approaches. We will also review several widgets in preparation for building our own later in the book. Then we will assess some of the more popular floater applications as well as explore a few hardware and software enhancements that can be used to further manipulate Android's standard application launching interface. Lastly, we will put all these pieces together to create an emulated Windows Phone or Mac desktop user experience running on an Android device.

2.1 Launchers

The stock home screen that comes on the standard Google Nexus devices offers a crisp, clean interface. But if you don't like how it looks or want to remove the Google search bar widget that refuses to budge when you try, you have several alternative approaches to choose from. These replacement home-screen layout and theme applications, called *launchers*, are available for download directly from the Google Play store. As the name implies, launchers can be used to launch applications. But they can also be used to customize everything from the look of icons to the transition animations that are displayed when moving between screens.

Some device manufacturers have created their own custom launchers to enhance and differentiate their Android devices. These include Samsung's TouchWiz[1] and HTC's Sense.[2] This degree of customization demonstrates a major advantage that Android has over competing mobile operating systems. This also helps to accelerate user experience innovations because Android offers a platform where experimentation is not only possible but embraced.

Most of the commercially available launchers offer a free version to play with that are either ad-banner supported, restricted in features, or constrained to a certain degree of customization. If customers like what they see, they are encouraged to reward the launcher's creator with a paid upgrade that will remove ads and/or unlock additional features. The nice thing about these commercial launchers is that they can easily be installed just like any other program that can be obtained from the Google Play store. Once downloaded and installed, the replacement launcher will ask for your permission to always be used as the default launcher. You can also choose to run a launcher once before making the launcher replacement a global change. At the time of this writing, the most popular launchers on Google Play are ADWLauncher EX,[3] Apex Launcher Pro,[4] GO Launcher EX,[5] and Nova Launcher Prime.[6] Let's take a brief look at each of these to see what they have to offer and what differentiates one from the other.

---

1. http://en.wikipedia.org/wiki/TouchWiz
2. http://en.wikipedia.org/wiki/HTC_Sense
3. https://play.google.com/store/apps/details?id=org.adwfreak.launcher
4. https://play.google.com/store/apps/details?id=com.anddoes.launcher.pro
5. https://play.google.com/store/apps/details?id=com.gau.go.launcherex
6. https://play.google.com/store/apps/details?id=com.teslacoilsw.launcher.prime

ADWLauncher EX

One of the most downloaded launchers on the market, ADWLauncher EX's main claim to fame is that it runs on platforms as far back as Android OS version 1.6. Even on that early Android release, ADWLauncher EX offers the same kind of eye candy and customization features found on later Android releases. However, maintaining this visual compatibility comes at the price of a slightly larger application installation size compared to other launchers.

Pros

- Runs on the Android operating systems as far back as version 1.6 (aka Donut)
- Fair number of customization options and graphical flourishes, such as page transitions, icon adjustments, and app organization styles

Cons

- Larger installation footprint compared to other third-party launchers
- Not yet optimized for Android 4.2 and newer
- Can be problematic with some widgets

Apex Launcher Pro

This launcher has become popular among the Android 4.0 crowd, partly because it doesn't run on any Android versions older than the 4.0 release. As such, the install footprint is tiny in comparison to something like ADWLauncher EX. Apex Launcher Pro can also use launcher themes created for competing launcher platforms like ADW and Go Launcher.

Pros

- Optimized for Android 4.0 and newer
- Tiny install footprint
- Can import themes from several competing third-party launchers

Cons

- More expensive than other third-party launchers
- Not quite bleeding edge, but good enough to take advantage of the latest themes and design aesthetics that Android 4.2 utilizes

GO Launcher EX

With more than a million installations since its release into the Play market-place, GO Launcher EX is by far the most popular on Google Play and has the largest variety of third-party add-ons and inventive creations formatted for the program's graphic templates. It's also free, but at a big price in the form of in-app advertising. While other launchers offer free, ad-supported versions, most of the alternatives offer a paid upgrade version that eliminates in-app advertising along with expanded graphic options.

Pros

- It's free.
- This is the most popular launcher on the market, with a thriving add-on and custom theme market (more than 5,000 and counting).
- It runs on Android 2.0 and newer.

Cons

- In-app push advertising clutters the experience.
- It doesn't consume themes built with other third-party launchers.

Nova Launcher Prime

TeslaCoil Software's Nova Launcher Prime (shown in the figure here) is one of the newest Android launcher programs on the market. Like Apex Launcher Pro, Nova Launcher Prime runs only on Android 4.0 and newer devices. As such, its minuscule install size coupled with its ability to import ADW or Go Launcher icon themes elevate it beyond a casual launcher replacement. It's one of the more expensive launchers analyzed in this chapter, but I find that it is also one of the most flexible and intuitively designed.

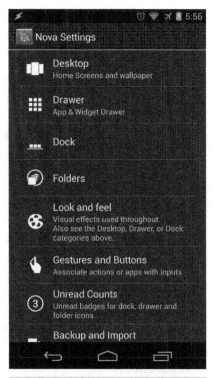

Nova Launcher Prime is my personal launcher of choice and the one I used throughout this book. And because this book assumes you are also using a device running Android OS 4.0 or newer, Nova Launcher Prime is an even easier top recommendation to make.

Figure 4—Nova Launcher Prime
is my preferred launcher.

Pros

- Optimized for the Android 4.0 user experience
- Flexible yet intuitive user interface options
- Can import and use ADW and Go Launcher icon themes
- Built-in unread count badges for Gmail, missed calls, and SMS

Cons

- Comparatively expensive

Who Can You Trust?

While these launchers offer a fun and visually exciting way to customize the look and feel of the home screen and icons that populate the screen, they require an extraordinary level of access to a number of areas within the Android operating system to do their magic. Even though a majority of Android applications usually need only two or three permissions (such as Internet access, read-write access to the SD card, and so on), several of the Android launchers featured in this chapter require a whole host of OS-level permissions, from reading your contacts, text messages, call log, and email to having full network access. Given such broad access to your data and a connection to a network, untrustworthy launchers could harvest that data for their own nefarious purposes.

Fortunately, it's unlikely that the more popular launchers highlighted in this book would be engaging in such practices since they are used by so many people; the likelihood is small that security-conscious customers using these products would be monitoring the application's network interaction for any funny business. Yet while companies that create these launchers are seeking commercial gain through the sale of their application, the more popular a launcher becomes, the more likely unscrupulous hackers could seek out and exploit security flaws in the launcher by exploiting unintentional vulnerabilities in the target launcher application.

The lesson to be learned with this array of launchers is that Google could step up its game and bake launcher customization within the Android OS. Not only will this alleviate security concerns (that these third-party launchers have unfettered access to so many sensitive areas of the phone or tablet), but it will also help to standardize on theme formats. Instead of being locked into one vendor's interpretation of what a launcher theme should consist of, Google could help set a universal protocol that Android users and independent theme designers could follow. Until then, we're stuck with entrusting these third-party providers with our device's security.

Launchers can be combined with custom wallpaper images, icons, and screen transitions to create a new level of personalized artistic expression among a new generation of mobile connected users. Just as car exteriors were customized during the mid-1960s through the '70s by that generation's youth, this design trend has been reborn in the mobile generation. Even more levels of customization can be realized using widgets. Let's take a closer look at this standout feature that is part of the Android OS experience.

2.2 Widgets

A major distinction between a desktop computer and a mobile OS such as Android is the way people interact with information on the display. A desktop offers considerably more screen real estate (even more so with multiple monitors) than is typically offered on a mobile display. As such, running dozens of windowed applications on a mobile device isn't very practical. Yet the power of a multitasking OS such as Android allows for many programs to be running at the same time.

Android has solved this constraint somewhat with the creation of widgets. *Widgets* are small graphical applications anchored to the home screen that can display data in a space as small as a single icon or expand to take over most of the screen. In this section, we'll take a look at how to select and use widgets, as well as sample a few of my favorite Android widgets.

When widgets were introduced in the early days of Android, they were one of the most defining features of the OS when compared to competing mobile platforms. Since then, widgets have found their niche as a collection of useful albeit limited views often for larger host applications.

For example, many media players available for sale on the Google Play store include widgets of various sizes that distill basic functions such as play/pause and forward/rewind onto screen areas that span anywhere from one-by-two to four-by-four tiles. Other widgets offer scrolling news-ticker-style updates from RSS feeds, server status, and to-do list reminders, among other things. In addition to the widgets available on the Google Play store, Android ships with its own collection of widgets to support the variety of Google applications on the phone.

Discovering the widgets installed on your Android device and adding a widget to your home screen is easy. To view the widgets installed on your phone on a standard Android 4.2 launcher configuration, select the Applications group icon from the lower center of the screen. This will display icons of all the visible programs on your device. From this screen, select the Widget tab to view the installed widgets as shown in Figure 5, *Android widgets selection screen*, on page 15.

Choose a widget by long-pressing the widget's icon. This will transform the icon into a floating representation that you can select and drag on your Android's home screen. Depending on the type of widget, a preference settings screen may appear after you have released the widget's floating icon for placement. This settings screen may be specific to that widget or, if the widget is a window to a full Android application, display the settings screen for that host program. And in Android 4.2 and newer, widgets can be resized to consume more or less space on the home screens. This flexibility adds an even higher degree of home-screen customization, allowing you to tweak exactly how you want your screen to appear.

Figure 5—Android widgets selection screen

Lock-Screen Widgets

While the original intent of the lock screen was to prevent the phone from accidentally launching apps or dialing numbers while jostling in your pocket, lock screens are increasingly important. Mobile devices have become containers of personal information, and the content should be protected with the same security applied in the physical world. But as security increases, convenience decreases. So, something as simple as checking your calendar can become a time-consuming dance of unlocking your phone, scrolling to the calendar icon, launching the program, scrolling to the appointment, and expanding the view for details.

To offset this kind of inconvenience, Google introduced a widget enhancement feature for the lock screen called, you guessed it, lock-screen widgets. The lock-screen widgets that are bundled in the standard Android 4.2 OS allow you to view items such as your calendar, email, and contacts and to even launch the Camera app without having to unlock the screen.

To select a lock-screen widget, swipe to the left while the lock screen is enabled. This will display a blank grid with a plus symbol in the center, as shown in Figure 6, *Adding widgets to the lock screen*, on page 16. Select the plus symbol, and a list of widgets that are lock screen–compliant will be displayed, as shown in Figure 7, *A selection of lock-screen widgets*, on page 16.

Scroll through the list to choose the one you want and place it on the lock screen via the same procedure as placing a regular widget on the home screen.

Figure 6—Adding widgets to the lock screen

Figure 7—A selection of lock-screen widgets

Considering the number of home-screen widgets available in the Google Play store, the choice of lock-screen widgets is not nearly as expansive. This is surprising considering how easy it is for developers to take existing widgets and convert them to be lock screen–compatible.

Perhaps as a result of this dearth of lock-screen widgets compared to home-screen widgets, Android engineer Roman Nurik created the DashClock widget.[7] This innovative replacement for the standard Android lock-screen clock application can host additional details in neatly defined groupings of information. DashClock also solves the problem, related to both home-screen and lock-screen widgets, of when your screens start filling up quickly, requiring you to scroll back and forth to look for quick tidbits of information.

---

7. https://play.google.com/store/apps/details?id=net.nurik.roman.dashclock

The other advantage that DashClock offers is a very easy way to hook into its API so that third-party data sources can be displayed in DashClock's container.[8] Roman released the DashClock source code under the open source Apache License 2.0, making it a hit among developers who have rewarded Roman's efforts with a thriving number of add-ons. These range from battery and dialing extensions to word-of-the-day and Facebook message counts.

Of course, with all these extensions, you have to be cautious about the type of lock-screen enhancements you install. As is the case with something like the Gmail or Calendar lock-screen widget, DashClock extensions might be exposing data that you don't want to display on a pocket billboard. DashClock also has access to permissions such as contacts, email, and location that can be polled by it and the extensions it hosts. So, unless you implicitly trust whatever extension you host within DashClock, be wary of what you install.

My Favorite Widgets

I try to keep my widget count to a minimum (see the figure here). Too many widgets, especially those polling for frequent network updates, can impact performance and battery life. I also stay away from the widgets with lots of graphical flourishes and large screen footprints because I find them distracting and overstepping their intention of quickly assessing the data they are trying to convey. That said, here are some of the widgets I prefer.

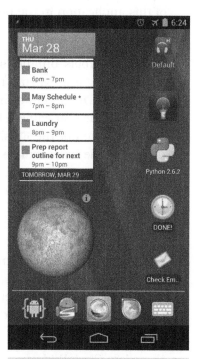

Figure 8—These are a few of my favorite things.

- *Calendar*

   This is the widget component of Google's calendar application that is included with Android running Google applications. It's helpful for taking a quick glance at upcoming scheduled events.

- *Moon Phase Pro*

   Being a child of the 1960s and having early memories of watching a blurry television screen showing Neil Armstrong step

---

8. http://code.google.com/p/dashclock/wiki/API

onto the surface of the moon has endeared me to all things space. Moon Phase Pro[9] created by developer Udell Enterprises keeps me in touch with my fascination with celestial bodies. In addition to the main program that displays the monthly phases of the moon along with other interesting statistics, the program comes bundled with several widgets of various sizes and levels of detail.

- *Headset Button Controller*

  I use this application each time I press the button on my Android headset. Created by Android developer Christoph Kober, Headset Button Controller essentially allows you to assign different actions to each type of headset button press.[10] Those actions can span from running scripts and applications to reassigning behaviors to other button presses. The program includes a widget that allows you to quickly switch between different headset button profiles. We will explore in greater detail and make use of this application in the next chapter.

- *Smart Tools Flashlight*

  The Smart Tools bundle is a helpful collection of fifteen measurement tools ranging from virtual rulers and protractors to metal detectors and magnifiers. The program includes a helpful Flashlight widget that turns on and off the rear camera light (if you have one on your phone or tablet) with the touch of the Flashlight widget icon. This has helped me more than a couple times while searching for keyholes and safe walkways and for paper-based reading at night. Since I always have my Android phone with me, I always have a flashlight with me as well thanks to this useful widget.

- *Python Interpreter*

  This widget provides a shortcut to the Python interpreter hosted within the Scripting Layer for Android (SL4A) program. Besides Python, SL4A can host a number of other different languages within the Android environment. We will learn much more about the SL4A in Chapter 5, *Scripting with SL4A*, on page 63.

- *Pomodoro Clock Widget*

  This is my second favorite widget and one I built myself. Touching this widget activates a Pomodoro countdown timer. I will tell you more about

---

9. https://play.google.com/store/apps/details?id=com.daylightmap.moon.pro.android
10. https://play.google.com/store/apps/details?id=com.kober.headsetbutton

Pomodoro timers and walk you through the process of building this widget in Chapter 7, *Tasker Pomodoro Widget*, on page 93.

• *Check Mail Widget*

This is my favorite widget and, like the Pomodoro Clock widget, is also one I built myself. When tapped, the Check Mail widget will check for new email and speak any new unread messages received. I find that this widget and the corresponding script it executes is crucial for the hands-free reporting of new mail messages. We will be building this widget and the backend script that powers it in Chapter 8, *Messaging Projects*, on page 115.

Now you should have a pretty good idea of the types of custom application launchers and widgets that Android has to offer. In the next section, we will take a look at a special type of Android application that gives your Android device a retro feel by harkening back to the days of traditional PC-based, window-driven GUIs.

2.3 Floaters

There is another category of Android applications that can be displayed on the screen within a movable window. I call these programs *floaters*. Floaters behave just like a window in a modern desktop computing OS. Most can be resized, minimized, and maximized, and some even support multiple instances, allowing multiple windows on the screen at the same time. See the figure here.

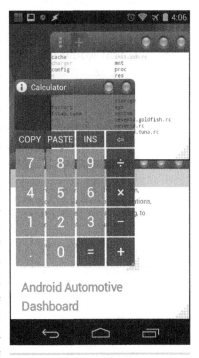

Figure 9—Several floaters in action

The advantages of using floaters are not as great as you might expect. They really don't work all that well on an Android phone with a small display. Screen real estate is already at a premium, and managing windows on top of an already limited overall display field can get annoying after a while. There's also the dissonance problem of merging an old GUI desktop application metaphor onto a modern mobile operating system. It breaks up the flow, and you may find yourself spending more time moving around and organizing windowed applications than actually interacting with the data they contain.

That said, there are a few benefits. Let's say you're watching a video and need to check and respond to email. Normally you would have to pause the playback to do so. Using a floater media player, you can just resize the window while perusing your messages and then expand the playback to full screen without missing a moment of content. There's also the coolness and geek credibility factors to be able to show colleagues something they might not have thought possible on a mobile device. Lastly, floaters work rather nicely on a 10-inch Android tablet thanks to the much larger screen size that gives you the ability to effortlessly move and resize windows. I tend to use floaters most frequently on these types of large-screen devices.

While quite a few floater-style applications are available in the Google Play store, here are a few worthy of a closer look:

- *AirCalc*[11]

  AirCalc is a simple yet free calculator for Android. It also provides a nice introduction to floaters and is a great way to determine whether your Android device supports the app screen overlay techniques employed by most floater programs. AirCalc can be resized, minimized, and maximized just as you would expect a traditional windowed application to behave.

- *AirTerm*[12]

  AirTerm is another program written by MBFG (short for My Boyfriend is a Geek), the same folks behind AirCalc and several other floaters available from the Google Play store. AirTerm incorporates KBOX,[13] a full-featured Busybox clone for nonrooted Android devices.[14] KBOX includes useful Unix-oriented command-line utilities such as scp, ssh, vim, wget, and more. While not as complete as something like Terminal IDE (refer to Appendix 1, *Android Programming Tools*, on page 187, for more information on this tremendously useful Android utility), AirTerm can help out in a pinch. I typically call upon AirTerm on my tablet when simultaneously administering several Linux servers at the same time.

---

11. https://play.google.com/store/apps/details?id=com.myboyfriendisageek.aircalc
12. https://play.google.com/store/apps/details?id=com.myboyfriendisageek.airterm
13. http://kevinboone.net/kbox.html
14. http://www.busybox.net

- *DICE Player*[15]

  DICE Player is a free (donations encouraged), full-featured media player
  for Android. In addition to supporting a variety of playback formats, DICE
  Player includes the ability to convert the normal full-screen playback
  mode into a floating pop-up player. The windowed player can be resized
  like any other floater-style application. One nifty aspect I like about the
  DICE Player is its ability to speed up playback without altering the pitch.
  This allows me to watch screencasts twice as fast without changing the
  pitch of the audio. A typical scenario on my tablet is to have DICE play
  back a screencast in double time while I have Terminal IDE or AirTerm
  open, interacting with a server running the configuration being presented
  in the screencast. It's the ultimate post-PC learning experience.

- *Overskreen*[16]

  Overskreen is another MBFG application that brings the floater technique
  to the standard Android web browser. Because of this, Overskreen is a
  no-frills browser that can't compete with the likes of Chrome or Firefox.
  Still, its floater properties come in handy when searching the Web or
  referring to a website while writing a document. It sure beats the alternative tap-and-swipe dance common when switching between running
  Android programs.

- *Stick it!*[17]

  Stick it! is another Android media player that, like DICE Player, provides
  video playback within a pop-up window. However, unlike DICE Player,
  Stick it! offers a neat feature on higher-end Android devices called Multi-
  View. This essentially allows for multiple windows to play back different
  video content at the same time. It's an awesome technology demo, but I
  honestly haven't used MultiView in many real-world scenarios. And as
  you can imagine, playing several videos at the same time can be rather
  taxing on your battery and system resources. But for a whiz-bang Android
  showcase program, Stick it! is hard to beat.

Now that we have all the visual customization tools and applications that we
need to have Android's home screen look and behave the way we want, let's
apply these ideas to re-create two home screens. One will emulate a competing

15. https://play.google.com/store/apps/details?id=com.inisoft.mediaplayer.a

16. https://play.google.com/store/apps/details?id=com.myboyfriendisageek.airbrowser

17. https://play.google.com/store/apps/details?id=com.myboyfriendisageek.stickit

phone operating system, and another will re-create the look and feel of a popular desktop operating system.

2.4 Home Screen Customization

Part of the fun of having the level of customization that Android allows is to re-create familiar computing metaphors. We're going to do just that with a quick walk-through of applying themes, widgets, and floaters to emulate the look and feel of an alternative mobile OS platform. The other will be the re-creation of a prevalent desktop operating system. Let's begin by emulating Microsoft Windows Phone.

Emulating the Windows Phone Look

Our first emulated home screen will be that of a Microsoft Windows Phone. Like many themes available for free download from Google Play, the GO Launcher EX Windows Phone 7 pays homage to the clean interface that the Windows Phone user interface offers.[18] While this theme doesn't completely redefine your Android's phone behavior to emulate a Windows Phone, it does provide a way to dress up the background and icons to give the appearance of a Windows Phone–inspired home screen.

If you're using the GO Launcher EX as your launcher of choice, installing this theme is a breeze. Simply download it from Google Play and select it from the list of themes in the Go Launcher preferences screen. On the other hand, if, like me, you've opted to use TeslaCoil's Nova Launcher Prime as your preferred Android launcher replacement, there are a few more steps you need to take to incorporate the graphical elements contained in this Windows Phone theme.

Configuring Nova Launcher Prime

After the theme has been downloaded, open Nova Launcher Prime's settings. Before you replace anything or alter your existing launcher settings, make a backup of your existing Nova Launcher Prime configuration by selecting the Backup and Import option. This will display the Backup and Import screen, as shown in Figure 10, *Nova Launcher Prime's Backup and Import screen*, on page 23.

Select the Backup label and name your backup or accept the default name of a date stamp for your backup file. Now if something unexpected should happen during the import of a new theme or you don't like the way the new theme looks, you can easily restore your current launcher layout and behavior.

---

18. https://play.google.com/store/apps/details?id=com.gau.go.launcherex.theme.wpsevenstyle

With a backup made, select the Import label from the Backup and Import screen. Nova Launcher Prime will remind you that your existing launcher settings will be replaced by the theme being imported. You know, the one you were supposed to make a backup of, right? Since you *do* have a backup of your current configuration, return to the Nova Settings screen and select the Look and Feel option. From there, choose the Icon Theme option. The list of the various themes installed on your Android device will be displayed, as shown in Figure 11, *A selection of installed icon themes.*

**Figure 10—Nova Launcher Prime's
Backup and Import screen**

**Figure 11—A selection of
installed icon themes**

Now we're going to use Nova Launcher Prime's ability to import icons from other launcher application themes. In this case, we will borrow some Windows Phone–like icons from a Windows 7 GO Launcher theme. Choose the GO Launcher EX Windows Phone 7 theme from the list. This will replace icons for standard Android programs such as Browser, Email, and Settings with a Windows Phone icon lookalike. Arrange your choice of applications on your home screen accordingly. Press and hold on the home-screen background to either change it to a solid color or incorporate a matching Android wallpaper. I prefer the live wallpaper that is installed with the Moon Phase Pro program.

Tinker with the layout until you achieve the look and feel you're comfortable with. When you're done, it may look similar to the one shown in Figure 12, *A Windows Phone theme*.

In the next example, we will use a free theme originally designed for ADW.Launcher and pull in its icon assets to reflect a popular desktop OS.

Emulating the OS X Desktop

For this next theme, you can either use the launcher it was initially designed for (ADW.Launcher) or use the icon import capability of Nova Launcher Prime, as we did in the previous example. And as before, it's always a good idea to make a backup of your existing settings in case something goes wrong or you want to return to your original launcher settings.

Install the ADW Theme MacOS Theme from Google Play.[19] Then, just as we did for the Windows Phone theme, go into Nova Launcher Prime's settings screen. Select the "Look and feel" option followed by the Icon Theme option. This will display a list of compatible themes that Nova Launcher Prime can use. Select the

Figure 12—A Windows Phone theme

ADW MacOS theme from the list. Doing so will replace some of the standard Android program icons with facsimiles of popular Mac OS X icons.

Next, replace the home screen's background wallpaper with a Mac desktop wallpaper. Launch the default Android or Google Chrome browser, search Google Images for "Mac desktop wallpaper,"[20] and select any of the ones that appeal to you. Set the image to your wallpaper by long-pressing the image of choice. A pop-up menu will appear, as shown in Figure 13, *Setting background wallpaper using an image from the Web*, on page 25.

Select the "Set as wallpaper" option. This will download the selected image, save it locally to your Android file storage, and set the image as the default home-screen background.

---

19. https://play.google.com/store/apps/details?id=akglo.themes.macos
20. https://images.google.com

With the background wallpaper set, create shortcuts to popular Android programs such as Browser, Email, and Settings on the home screen. Complete the effect by running a floater application like Stick it! to give the home screen the look and feel of a mini OS X desktop computer, as shown in Figure 14, *Recreation of the OS X desktop*, on page 26.

Making Your Own Home Screen

Now that you have an idea how to apply existing themes to re-create familiar desktop platforms, try making your own themes using a similar approach. Go retro and re-create a Commodore Amiga or Atari ST desktop on your Android. How about blending several desktop metaphors into your own unique creation? Depending on how artistic you are, you can even create your own background and icon images based on a favorite interest or hobby. Android allows you to explore and apply your ideas at your leisure.

Figure 13—Setting background wallpaper using an image from the Web

2.5 Next Steps

This chapter showed just how easy it is to customize the Android graphical user experience to your liking. Whether it's embracing the mobile lifestyle to the fullest or harkening back to a legacy PC user experience, Android gives you the freedom to choose how you want the interface to look and behave. This is a significant advantage, especially compared to platforms like those powered by Apple iOS. Android allows you to express yourself without jailbreaking or rooting your device, something that might be required to do to achieve the same effect on other mobile platforms.

Now that you have the knowledge and the tools to customize your Android device the way you see fit, explore the numerous themes available for download. If you're using TeslaCoil's Nova Launcher Prime, you will find that most background and icon themes are compatible. However, most graphical embellishment behaviors that accompany these themes, especially those written for Go Launcher, don't work as expected, if at all. Still, there are hundreds of freely available themes to choose from, and that number is expanding every day. If you don't find one you like, you can create your own

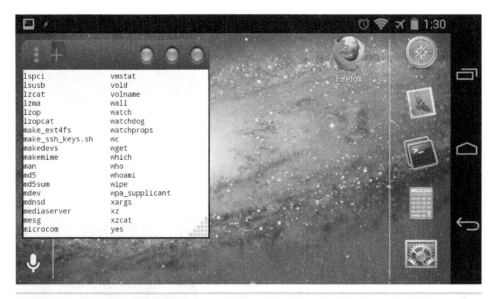

Figure 14—Re-creation of the OS X desktop

by converting pictures you took with your Android's camera into home-screen backgrounds and icons. Your first attempts might not be works of art, but they will most definitely express what you want your mobile computing experience to look like!

In the next chapter, we will explore how to customize the other side of the user experience by focusing on audio. Specifically, we will learn how to leverage audio in Android to augment and in some cases even replace the Android user interface. Get ready to listen up!

CHAPTER 3

Listening to Your Android

Customizing your home screen's look and behavior is visually stimulating, but there are so many other facets of Android that allow it to be personalized. In this chapter, we'll take a look at interacting with the information that your Android device can deliver.

For example, did you know that your Android can speak to you? Ever since the Android 1.6 OS release, Android has had built-in text-to-speech (TTS) functionality that could convert text into spoken words. However, it wasn't until the release of Android 4.2 that this TTS technology was actually tolerable to listen to for long stretches. Earlier releases were robotic and lifeless. The 4.2 release includes a far more natural and less obnoxious voice. And if this default voice isn't to your liking, third-party text-to-speech synthesis products like those from SVOX offer a selection of more than forty voices in multiple languages.[1] Before 4.2 came along, I used SVOX for my TTS needs.

But before we get to hear our phone, we should optimize our listening environment for on-the-go audio data consumption.

3.1 Wearable Computing

With all the recent interest in wearable computing, people often forget that an Android phone already *is* a wearable computer. I have been using my Android phone as a wearable computing device for years. Let me explain.

The term *wearable computer* has a broad definition applying to everything from a wristwatch to a powered laptop strapped to a backpack. In terms of my Android phone, I wear it in a case attached to my belt loop. However, rather than reaching for the phone every time I hear its message chime, I have written scripts and applications that inform me of those messages

---

1. https://play.google.com/store/apps/details?id=com.svox.classic

without ever having to remove the phone from its case. Email, text messages, meeting notifications, countdown timers, motivational reminders, and other information are controlled and delivered via my audio headset.

This chapter will show you how to put the pieces into place to allow you to do the same thing. The setup is simple and inexpensive. And unlike Google's much hyped and considerably more expensive Glass project, my Android wearable configuration doesn't obstruct or distract my vision in any way.

Many people prefer to put their smartphones in their pocket, but I find it far easier to use a wired headset when the device is holstered in a case strapped to my belt. I prefer the Case Logic TBC-412 model. Even though this product is officially designated as a video camera case, I find that it snuggly fits my Galaxy Nexus even with the added thickness of a 3850mAh extra-capacity battery. It also protects the phone from the elements, whether that is a drizzle of rain or a dusty biking trail. The price is also cheaper than custom-designed slip cases made specifically for the phone.

With the phone safely enclosed, run a headphone wire from your shoulders to the phone. You can run the wire between layers of clothing to keep it out of the way. Some headsets come with a helpful plastic clip that allows you to put some slack into the wire. That keeps the earphones from tugging at your ears. I attach this clip to my shirt collar to keep the left and right earphone wires from slipping as I walk. The headphones I use on a daily basis are a cheap single-button design with a built-in mic that is compatible with most Samsung Galaxy phone models. These can often be found on Amazon for as low as a dollar plus shipping. Note that the headset you use must have a headset button, since you will use that button to answer calls, start and stop audio, and run applications.

You can opt for a more expensive headset or earphones tailored to your phone hardware. You can also choose to go entirely wireless via a Bluetooth headset. But I have found from years of using my wearable configuration that these choices produce annoyances. For expensive wired headsets, I find that the wire at the stem of the headphone jack becomes weak over time and eventually loses either the left or right ear connection. I have even tried shielding the wire from this wear and tear by looping the wire at the stem of the headphone jack and tightly wrapping it with electrical tape to no avail.

As for Bluetooth headsets, I find that the sound quality still hasn't quite matched the frequency ranges offered by wired headsets. There is also the hassle of having to recharge the Bluetooth headset's battery before use. And it can be a pain when that charge dies midway through the day without having the means to recharge it until you're home.

If you choose a wired approach, you need to manage the path of the wires from your ears to your encased Android. Depending on the type of activity, you can try running the wire in between your outer and undershirts, either in front or back of you. Gadget-friendly clothing from progressive fashion designers like ScottEVest includes shirts and jackets with dedicated enclosures to run headphone wiring through so as not to flop around and get in your way.[2]

After spending a wad of cash on replacing expensive earphones and wireless headsets, I have reverted to cheap, throwaway headsets. They sound fine and offer nearly the same level of durability as more expensive alternatives yet at a far lower replacement cost.

With the headphones in place and the headphone button in a location that is easy access, you can use this button to control the basic features of the phone. Answer an incoming phone call as well as pause and play music with a single short press of the center headphone button. The basic button press behaviors are more or less universal across all Android phones that support headset controls.

With your Android by your side and your audio headset on, let's next turn our focus to the software involved in voice recognition and spoken text inter-action.

3.2 The Sound of Data

Before we can have Android speak to us, we first need to give it a voice. Setting up TTS on Android 4.2 and newer is easy. Select the "Language & input" option in the Settings program, then scroll down and select the "Text-to-speech output" item. This will display the text-to-speech output settings shown in Figure 15, *Text-to-speech output settings*, on page 30.

The default preferred speech engine in Android 4.2 is Google's own TTS technology. If you have SVOX or another third-party engine installed, it will also be listed on this settings page. From this screen, you can also modify the rate of speech playback, ranging from very slow to very fast. I prefer the default normal speed, but try each setting to see which of the five playback speeds works best for you. Select the "Listen to an example" option to hear

---

2.   http://www.scottevest.com

Android speak at the playback speed you chose. And now that we know Android can talk, let's explore how we can talk back to Android.

Running Android 4.2 and newer, you can hold down the earphone button for about a second, and the Google Now service will pop up,[3] ready to submit your query to Google for processing. In addition to submitting who, when, what, where, why, and how questions to Google's search engine, you can also command certain aspects of the phone by voicing key phrases, such as the following:

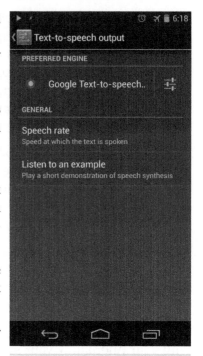

Figure 15—Text-to-speech output settings

- "Call <contact>" will locate the contact name most closely matching your spoken entry and place a phone call to that contact.

- "Listen to <track>" will play back the requested music track using the default music player.

- "Go to <URL>" will open a web browser and display the requested URL.

- "Open app <app name>" will launch the application, assuming it is installed on your device.

- "What time is it?" will display the time.

- "Set an alarm for <time>" will set an alarm to sound at the requested time.

- "Remind me to <task> at <time>" will convert your speech to text and add the converted statement to your default calendar at the designated time on the current day.

- "Navigate to <destination>" will map a route from your current location to your stated destination.

So, that's pretty cool, but Google Now has two notable drawbacks. First, while Google's voice recognition and speech-to-text translation services are amazing,

---

3. http://www.google.com/landing/now/

they're far from perfect. Try any of these phrases on a noisy bus or outside on a windy day, and you're not likely to see the results you expected.

Second, Google Now requires an Internet connection to work. That's right. If you want to play a song that is already stored on your device, ask to open an application, or play a music track, Google Now has to submit your converted speech-to-text request to its web service for these things to happen.

You would think that's because Google needs its server farm to chew through your speech input, convert it to a text string, and figure out the meaning of the submitted phrase. But that doesn't explain why Google offers offline speech-to-text translation in Android 4.2 and newer. Until Google creates an API that allows developers to access this offline speech-to-text translation service, developers need to continue submitting spoken phrases over the Internet to Google's servers.

The takeaway from all this is that if you live and commute in a well-connected city where wireless Internet connectivity is trustworthy, fast, and ubiquitous and you're not concerned about the voiceprint data Google is collecting from your audible queries, then Google Now can be mighty helpful at times. But while Google Now does a good job of translating responses such as the time and reminders into audio, most answers require looking at the screen to review the replies.

When I'm on the go, whether walking crowded city streets to work or riding my recumbent along winding bike trails, I really don't want to pull my phone out of my pocket to see who sent me a text message and what they said, view any upcoming events on my calendar, or simply check the time.

Fortunately, several hardworking Android developers have created applications that address these needs. Let's take a closer look at some of my favorites.

Talking SMS and Caller ID

Talking SMS and Caller ID offer hands-free text-to-speech announcements of inbound text messages and calls.[4] Knowing that you won't miss an impor-tant message or wonder whether the call you're receiving is from someone worth stopping to talk to is a nice anxiety dissipater. When you accept the application's permissions, it has complete access to your contacts list. If an inbound caller's phone number isn't associated with an existing contact, the program will read the phone number instead. If an SMS is received from an unknown contact, it won't bother reading the message (kind of nice when

---

4. https://play.google.com/store/apps/details?id=mahmed.net.spokencallername

minimizing SMS spam). It also doesn't consume a lot of system resources while running in the background awaiting a call or SMS to trigger it into action.

Talking Calendar

One of my biggest frustrations with program audio cues is that they provide only part of the story. Let's say you use a custom chime whenever a calendar reminder is triggered. Instead of knowing exactly what event is coming up, you have to stop whatever you were doing, dig out your phone, unlock the screen, flick down the notification bar, and parse through the various notifications just to figure out what's going on.

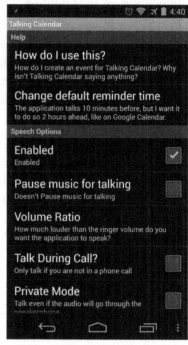

Talking Calendar eliminates this hassle by actually speaking the event to you instead.[5]

Talking Calendar, shown in Figure 16, *Configuring Talking Calendar*, hooks into not only your Google Calendar but your Exchange and CalDAV-formatted calendars as well, which is perfect for those who prefer to keep work-life and home-life events separate. The application is also smart enough to pause whatever audio might be playing long enough to read (via text-to-speech) the calendar event.

Figure 16—Configuring Talking Calendar

Android Voice Xtreme

The Google Play store has several other TTS-enabled applications, some of which compete with the ones I've already mentioned. But only one is what I label as the kitchen sink of speech recognition text-to-speech extravaganzas. As of the publication date of this book, Bulletproof's Android Voice Xtreme (AVX) is one of the most comprehensive and expensive voice-driven applications for sale on Google Play.[6] In addition to capturing and speaking text messages and caller IDs, it can also read email messages and integrate with third-party applications such as Google Hangouts (formerly known as Google Talk) and Evernote, among other things.

---

5.   https://play.google.com/store/apps/details?id=com.pwnwithyourphone.talkingcalendar
6.   https://play.google.com/store/apps/details?id=com.bulletproof.voicerec.avx

The main drawbacks of AVX are that it relies on an Internet connection to interpret speech-to-text entries and it consumes a hunk of system resources. It is also not the peppiest-performing Android commercial application either. Even more notable is that, because of the program's broad capabilities to interact with your Android device on so many levels, AVX also requests access to a number of permissions on your device. Approach with caution.

Once you have these hands-free utilities loaded and working, you'll quickly discover that they are great for incoming information and events, but they either can't send outbound messages or don't do so very well. There are a couple of reasons for this deficiency. The most obvious problem is lack of a proven input mechanic like an onscreen keyboard. We have already discussed the problems with speech-to-text conversion. Until Google opens up its offline speech translation engine API to developers, this will continue to be an issue. And even with access to this API, speech recognition degrades considerably in a noisy environment. If you have an active lifestyle, you're probably interacting and commuting in a noisy environment most of the time. But all is not lost. Button presses to the rescue!

3.3   Button Control

As I write this chapter, Google is ramping up hype for its impending release of Google Glass, its self-proclaimed game-changing wearable-computing device. Having been professionally around the computing block for nearly thirty years, I have seen the rise and fall of a variety of devices. I worked with Windows CE-powered wearable-computing head-mounted displays over a decade ago, and while it was a thrill developing applications on bleeding-edge technology at the time, those types of displays ultimately lost their luster for me. Why?

The most notable reasons are centered around eyestrain, obstructed views, and the uncomfortable feeling of a headband gradually making a dent into my forehead. While I still fantasize for the day when I can walk around like a futuristic superhero with total situational awareness, swirling graphics, flagging call-outs, and an always-on voice assistant ready to immediately act upon my lazy utterances, we still have a long way to go technologically before those science-fiction visions are fully realized. But while it's fun to dream of the future, I need an unobtrusive working solution today without all the annoyances I've already encountered.

Headset Button Controller,[7] created by Android developer Christoph Kober, has become my control interface of choice. This helpful piece of software allows you to assign tasks, scripts, and applications to execute on your phone with a click of your built-in headset button. I have assigned it to execute all of my hands-free, vision-free automation tasks, from telling me the time and current battery charge level of my device to checking for new email messages and Twitter posts. And because text-to-speech technology has improved so much in the last few years, hearing your phone or tablet read you lengthy passages of content isn't as monotonous as it sounds.

So Long, Long Button Press

Prior to the release of Android 4.2, Headset Button Controller provided considerably more flexibility and button press combinations to assign tasks and trigger actions. Unfortunately, the long press headset button event is no longer an option in Android 4.2 and newer. That's because Google has now reserved that single long-click action to launching Google Now from a headset. Even if you attempted a long press after a series of short presses, Google steps in as soon as that long press is recognized and takes over. By doing so, Google has severely constrained Headset Button Controller's combination of buttons to essentially four assignments for single-button headsets (plus two more for the headset plug-in and unplug events) and up to sixteen (along with the plug-in and unplug assignments) for those devices that include a volume control along with the middle button (since there can be up to four short-press assignments per button).

Google intended to capture the long-press headset button event to offer a consistent behavior across devices using Android 4.2 and newer. But forcing this upon all users without the ability to disable or reassign to a different button combination seems a tad heavy-handed. I hope Google will allow users to customize this choice in future iterations of the operating system, but for now we have to accept this imposed constraint.

As odd as it sounds, I look forward to hearing the synthetic female voice used as the default TTS engine in Android 4.2. It's nice to know that she's always there, keeping me informed of appointments, messages, to-dos, and directions. And like Aladdin rubbing a lamp to wake the genie, I use my assigned clicks interpreted by Headset Button Controller to instantiate a variety of automated workflows. Some of these workflows will be described in later chapters. But for now, think of the variety of click combinations to launch applications as a terse subset of Morse Code. One click to pause, two clicks to fast-forward, three to report time and battery life, and four to check email. We'll talk more about the last two custom programs in that click list later in the book.

---

7.   https://play.google.com/store/apps/details?id=com.kober.headsetbutton

Before purchasing the commercial version of Headset Button Controller, it's best to test the trial version to verify compatibility with your Android device. You will also need a headset with at least one inline button that you can use to initiate click events.

For example, my Galaxy Nexus phone supports only a single button headset, leaving me with a total of six actions I can assign to Headset Button Controller. So, grab your Android phone, plug in a compatible headset, install the trial edition of the button controller software, and let's configure it to launch the standard Android web browser when three headset button presses are detected.

Configuring the Headset Button

Before we can use the Headset Button Controller, we first need to configure it. Launch the Headset Button Controller program and select the easy tab, as shown in the figure here.

For our test, we will assign an action to open the web browser application. Select the "Triple click" option on the screen. This will display a dialog of various commands that can be assigned to that action, as shown in Figure 18, *Headset Button Controller easy tab*, on page 36.

Select the "Launch app" option. Doing so will display a list of applications installed on your device. Choose the Browser application. An alert like the one shown in Figure 19, *Allowing Android to wake up when launching a task*, on page 36, will pop up asking whether you want your phone to wake up when the launch action is started.

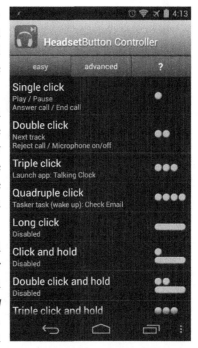

Figure 17—Headset Button Controller easy tab

Choosing to wake the phone when the action is initiated will turn on the screen and wake up the WiFi or cellular radios if they were in a low-power state. This way, when your browser's assigned home page is requested, the screen will be visible, and the network will be actively retrieving the content.

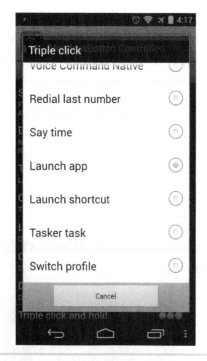

Figure 18—Headset Button Controller
easy tab

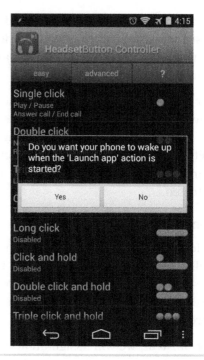

Figure 19—Allowing Android to wake up
when launching a task

Operating the Headset Button

If you haven't already done so, plug your headset into your Android device and triple-click the headphone's center button. As long as your headset hardware is compatible with the Headset Button Controller program, this action should launch and display the web browser. Congratulations, you now have the ability to initiate events without ever having to touch your phone's screen. This action will work whether or not your Android's screen is locked. We will leverage this newfound power to instantiate scripts and programs we will write later in the book.

Keep in mind that we can still use other applications that react to headset button presses while Headset Button Controller is running. You can have the program send button presses to a specific application (such as an audio player) or to whatever media player had been most recently used.

The most popular scenarios that have been enhanced by using the Headset Button Controller are for managing audio playback while listening to audiobooks, music, and podcasts. For example, you can control audio playback using commercial applications like Alex Kravchencko's Smart AudioBook Player (shown in the figure here),[8] or the DoggCatcher podcast program can be controlled entirely from the headset button.[9] A single click will pause and play the audio. Need to skip over boring commentary? Assign that action to a double-click of the headset button.

Figure 20—The smart audiobook player

Headset Button Controller even has a built-in speak-the-time function using Android's text-to-speech feature, but I find the program's implementation somewhat lacking. Consequently, I wrote my own talking clock application that I have assigned to a triple-click of the headset button. We will walk through the creation of this program and its configuration with Headset Button Controller in later chapters.

Distraction-free applications like the Headset Button Controller do a remarkable job of relieving you from having to fumble with your phone every time you want to skip over a song, answer a call, or check the time. It also elevates your phone to wearable-computing status as you realize how, using the right mix of applications and workflows, a good deal of information can be processed without ever having to look at a display. It's quite a liberating feeling as you become more skilled with this level of audio-delivered information optimization.

3.4 Next Steps

In this chapter, we learned about wearable computing and how it relates to today's Android devices. To that effect, we learned how to give Android smartphones and tablets a voice by enabling Android's text-to-speech capability. We also discovered how several commercially available Android programs take advantage of this built-in feature. And we configured a useful utility that

---

8. https://play.google.com/store/apps/details?id=ak.alizandro.smartaudiobookplayer
9. https://play.google.com/store/apps/details?id=com.snoggdoggler.android.applications.doggcatcher.v1_0

Soldering More Buttons

After getting over the dismay of losing the ability to reassign a single long press headset button in Android 4.2, I came across a post on the excellent Instructables.com website that reexpanded my options.[a] While I can only vouch for the effectiveness of the Galaxy Nexus, the author of the instructions indicates that it should work with other Android phones as well.

The idea is to take an inexpensive three-button inline remote designed for Apple products like the iPod touch or iPhone (the article suggests the iLuv iEA15BLK). Open the button casing, solder in two tiny resistors, and you can triple your Headset button options as a result.

The procedure does require soldering skills, steady hands, and good eyesight to be able to set the spec-sized resistors in place, but it worked like a charm for me and gave me another sixteen actions to assign to running various programs and tasks. If you enjoy tinkering with hardware and have the right equipment, try this approach.

Many thanks to my good friend and tech extraordinaire John Winans for use of his top-notch soldering equipment and laser-eye soldering technique. I couldn't have verified that this Instructables technique worked without his help.

---

a.   http://www.instructables.com/id/Galaxy-Nexus-and-others-headset-remote-with-medi/

gives us the ability to initiate actions on an Android smartphone with the click of a headset button.

Speaking of the headset button, take some time to explore your own application assignments for Headset Button Controller. Couple its functionality with the audio-oriented informational and productivity programs suggested in this chapter. As you reorient yourself toward a more audio-centric mobile lifestyle, consider the data that you would like to bring to your attention and have spoken to you. You will be able to put those ideas into action because we will soon learn how to automate workflow tasks and write custom scripts and programs that help process and deliver this data.

In the next section, we will put the sonic configuration promoted in this chapter to good use. We will construct a talking clock that will speak the time every fifteen minutes or whenever a triple-click is received by an attached headset button.

Part II

Explore

CHAPTER 4

Automating with Tasker

You can create sophisticated programs on Android that do what you want, when you want, all without having to learn anything about the Java language or the Android SDK. Better yet, you can wire up these programs using simple dialogs and icons that represent all the major functions that your Android device can do. In this chapter, I will show you how to do so with a little help from an Android program called Tasker.[1]

Tasker provides the ability to easily define and execute powerfully scripted actions that can be triggered by application, time, location, state, and event changes. With it, you could create a simple task that would automatically change the screen orientation to landscape and turn on the GPS radio whenever you launched a favorite navigation utility. You can also create more complex programs by linking together dozens of tasks. Tasker even has the ability to compile your programs so they can be freely executed on other Android devices that don't even have Tasker installed on them. Let's take a closer look at this popular and versatile workflow automation utility.

4.1 Introducing Tasker

Available for purchase from the Google Play marketplace for only a couple of dollars, Tasker centers around the ability to define tasks that execute a set of predefined actions to take when certain conditions are met. This can be something as simple as putting the phone into Airplane mode at bedtime or as complex as having your phone autonomously send your family a text message containing a Google Map link of your location when you reach a destination.

---

1.   http://tasker.dinglisch.net

Of all the apps I use on a new Android device, Tasker is consistently the first one I install. Tasker was written by developer Lee Wilmot during the early days of Android. Google was enticing new developers to the platform via prize-winning programming competitions called Android Developer Challenges, and Tasker was one of the finalists in that competition.

Tasker is somewhat equivalent to Apple's Automator on OS X, and while Tasker's user interface is in need of a makeover, the power imparted by the sophisticated scripts it can execute is unparalleled. Tasker exposes nearly every part of the addressable hardware and event-oriented portions of the operating system, making it relatively easy for people to configure their phones to certain triggers and respond to certain events.

How Tasker Works

Tasker offers the ability to run a series of tasks that you define based on several triggering criteria. Check out the figure here for examples of some of the individual tasks I created on my smartphone.

Task triggers can range from time and events to location or device state, such as an orientation change or headphone plug insertion. We will take a look at some of these trigger contexts in the example Tasker profiles we create in this chapter.

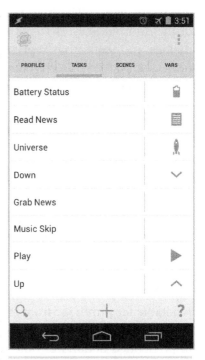

Installation and Configuration

Search the Google Play store for Tasker and click the Purchase button to buy and download the application to your Android device. Before approving the transaction, note the large number of permissions required by Tasker. This should come as no surprise given what is required for Tasker to run such a variety of hardware- and software-accessible functions.

Figure 21—A listing of custom Tasker tasks

Once installed, launch Tasker and take a look at the variety of parameters that can be changed via the UI, Monitor, Action, and Misc Preference tabs. For example, you can tweak the polling frequency of your current location coordinates more frequently than the default thirty seconds by modifying the value, as shown in the following figure. Note that all screenshots of Tasker shown in this book are from Tasker 4.0 installed on a Galaxy Nexus or Nexus 7 running Android 4.2. Tasker 4.0 incorporates Google's Holo theme. Prior versions of Tasker can run on devices running older versions of Android. However, since Holo is natively supported only on Android 4.*x* and newer versions of the operating system, Tasker's screens will look somewhat different on those older platforms. The good news is that the placement of dialog elements and Tasker's core functionality are mostly the same between platforms.

After you have become acquainted with the bevy of settings and polling frequencies that can be customized, exit the Preferences screen and switch to the Profiles tab. Profiles are used to organize various tasks under a single set to execute when a predefined condition is met. If you created a task to turn on the GPS radio and another task to sound an alarm when a desired location condition is met, you can combine these two tasks under a single profile. There are two major advantages to doing this. First, you can easily activate and deactivate a set of tasks to be run as needed. Second, you can reuse individually defined tasks in other profiles without having to reinvent and version control the same task routine over and over.

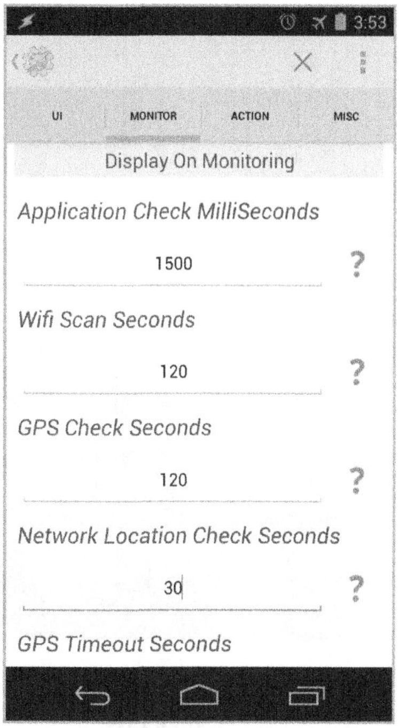

In the next section, we will put these ideas of tasks and profiles to use for our first Tasker program, a talking clock.

Figure 22—Network Location
Check Seconds field on
the Monitor tab

4.2 Talking Clock

The goal of this task is to automatically speak the time every fifteen minutes using Android's built-in text-to-speech (TTS) engine. Once we get the clock task working, we will create a second task that announces the device's current battery charge percentage at the top of every hour. We also don't want our clock to be waking us up every fifteen minutes while we're sleeping, so we will define in the profile the time frame for when the talking clock and battery tasks should run.

Launch Tasker and select the Tasks tab (as shown in Figure 23, *Creating a new task*, on page 44) by selecting the center plus icon in the bottom toolbar.

Type in *Say Time* as the new task name and touch the check mark to accept the name. Doing so will present you with an empty Task Edit screen that you can add new discrete tasks to. Select the center plus icon in the lower toolbar to add a new action to the task. This will display the dialog shown in Figure 24, *Tasker's Select Action Category dialog*, providing a list of more than twenty action categories to choose from.

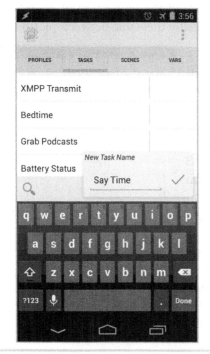

Figure 23—Creating a new task

Figure 24—Tasker's Select Action Category dialog

Select the Misc button, which features a question mark icon, and then select the Say button from the Select Misc Action dialog. This will display the Say form that allows us to manipulate a number of options, from what text to say and the voice engine to use to the speed and pitch of the text-to-speech playback. Select the gray tag icon to the upper right of the Text entry box. This will pop up a list that allows you to select from both Tasker's built-in variables as well as ones you have created (Figure 25, *Variable Select dialog*, on page 45).

Scroll down the list until you see the Time variable. Select it, and notice that Tasker populates the Text textbox with a predefined built-in variable called

Tasker Variables

Tasker has three types of variables: local, global, and built-in. Local variables are identified by all-lowercase variable names, such as %my_local_variable. Local variables are accessible only within the scope of a single task, and their values cannot be read by other tasks. Global variables are identified by the first letter in their names being uppercase, such as %My_global_variable. These can be read by any task created in Tasker and are useful for storing values that need to remain persistent and accessible across multiple tasks. The last type of Tasker variable are the built-in variables, such as %TIME, %GPS, %ROOT, and %WIFI. For a complete list of Tasker's built-in variable names, visit the Tasker website.[a]

---

a.   http://tasker.dinglisch.net/userguide/en/variables.html

%TIME. Next, assign the voice engine you want to use to speak the time by selecting the magnifying glass icon to the upper right of the Engine:Voice label. This will display a list of the various speech engines installed on the phone, such as Pico, SVOX,[2] or Google's own text-to-speech engine. Select your engine of choice.

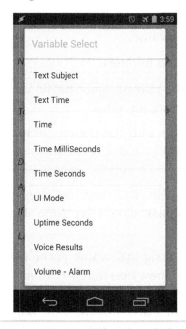

Figure 25—Variable Select dialog

Figure 26—Tasker Say options dialog

---

2.   https://play.google.com/store/apps/details?id=com.svox.classic

The Stream field allows you to assign the audio output to Android's Call, System, Ringer, Media, Alarm, and Notification audio channels. Choose the default "Media stream" option and leave Pitch and Speed at their midpoint default values, as shown in Figure 26, *Tasker Say options dialog*, on page 45.

Now that the Say action has been defined with what we want our phone to say and how to say it, select the Action Edit label located on the upper-left toolbar. This will save the first step in our Say Time task. Test the results by selecting the Play icon in the lower-right corner of the dialog box. You should hear your Android phone or tablet speak the current time in 24-hour format.

As an example, if it's 4:22 p.m. when you run the task, your phone will say "Sixteen point two two." Well, that's literally the time but not the common North American way of speaking it. Let's fix that.

Enhancing the Clock

We could just keep the spoken time format of the talking clock as is, but I prefer a traditional 12-hour reading that indicates morning (a.m.) or afternoon/evening (p.m.). To convert the 24-hour clock to a 12-hour reading, we have to do the following:

1. Create a variable to hold the current time value.

2. Split the current time string into hours and minutes.

3. Determine whether it's a.m. or p.m. If the current hour on the 24-hour clock is greater than 11, it's p.m. Otherwise, it's a.m.

4. Take into account zero-hour substitutions with the phrase "o'clock" so that when the clock strikes 5 a.m., it says "Five o'clock A-M" and not "Five zero A-M."

5. The same goes for any minutes announcements less than 10. For example, if the time is 9:07 p.m., the Talking Clock task should say "Nine oh seven P-M" and not "Nine zero seven P-M."

The first thing we need to do is create and assign the value of the built-in %TIME variable to a local variable (let's call it %current_time) that we can manipulate. Select the Say Time task we created earlier. Delete the action we created for the original Say Time task by long-selecting (i.e., holding your finger on the selection for at least two seconds). Choose Cut from the Action Options pop-up menu. Then create the new first step in the task list by selecting the center plus icon from Tasker's bottom toolbar. The Variable Select dialog will once again be displayed. Select the Variable category from the Action Category dialog, followed by the Variable Set action from this Variable pop-up dialog box. This will pop up a Variable Set dialog. Set the name of one of the new variables we will create for this task to %current_time and assign it to the built-in %TIME variable that we called upon earlier. Save the step by selecting the Action Edit label in the left of Tasker's top toolbar.

Next, we need to split this captured %current_time value into hours and minutes. This is done by creating a new step using Tasker's Variable Split function. Choose this function from the Variable action category like we did for the first Variable Set step. The Variable Split task function works by splitting the variable passed to it into two or more elements based on the delimiter chosen. In the case of %current_time, this delimiter is a period, so enter that character into the Splitter field. When Tasker executes a Variable Split task, it will incrementally number the original variable name and assign the split values accordingly. So, when the Variable Split function is applied to the %current_time variable, Tasker separates it between the period character into hours and minutes. Tasker will generate a %current_time1 and %current_time2 to hold the newly split values of hours and minutes, respectively. Save this action and continue.

We could leave the split variable names %current_time1 and %current_time2, but that may be confusing should we need to revisit or modify the script later. So, let's give them the appropriate names of %current_hour and %current_minute, respectively. Just as before, choose Tasker's Variable Set action from the Action Category -> Variable dialog. Once completed, you should have four action steps created in your Say Time task.

Now let's determine whether it's a.m. or p.m. If the 24-hour value is less than twelve, it's a.m. If it's greater than eleven, it's p.m. Once again, call upon Variable Set action, name the variable %am_pm, and then scroll down the Variable Set form to the If field. Add the condition If %current_hour < 12. Since this is a mathematical operation, select the Maths: Less Than choice from the Select Conditional Operator menu accessed by tapping the gray tag icon in the If row of the form. Once defined, the screen should look like Figure 27, *Variable Set form for the %am_pm variable*, on page 48.

Do a similar type of operation for creating and setting the %am_pm variable to p.m. if %current_hour is greater than eleven, as shown in Figure 28, *Select Task Action dialog*, on page 48.

You may be wondering why I didn't just create the %am_pm and use If and Else actions from Tasker's Task Action options. Simple—I'm lazy. My initial construction accomplished the same objective in fewer steps.

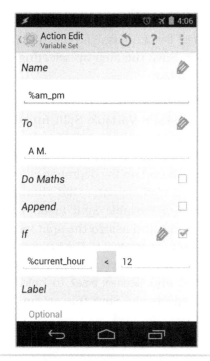

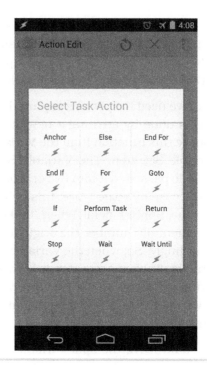

Figure 27—Variable Set form for the %am_pm variable

Figure 28—Select Task Action dialog

We now have the current hour, minute, and a.m. or p.m. values, but if we were to stop at this point, we would have a few problems. First, we want the clock to read a 12-hour, not 24-hour, time clock. The existing version will read midnight as "Zero A-M" and not the more appropriate "12 A-M." If the time is 11 p.m, we want our clock to say "Eleven o'clock P-M" and not "Twenty three zero P-M." And as the example error shows, we also need to account for substituting a zero minute value with the more appropriate "oh" sound. Lastly, we need to test for the condition when it is the top of the hour so that we can append the word *clock* during the read.

We will fix the midnight problem by setting the %current_hour variable to 12 if the %current_hour is equal to 0. Next, subtract 12 from the %current_hour if the %current_hour is greater than 12. These two actions properly set the hour reading value for a 12-hour clock.

Only a few more steps to go before our talking clock task is complete.

Let's now take care of the "oh" sound by setting a new variable that we'll call %say_oh to the "oh" string. We will also need to add a step that will check to see whether we need to include the "oh" in the time reading. You need to say the "oh" word only when substituting for a zero in the second place of the minutes field, such as 00 through 09. As such, we should omit an inserted "oh" word for any minutes greater than nine minutes after the hour. To do so, add another Variable Set step that sets the %say_oh variable to an empty string If %current_minute is greater than nine.

Now let's address the top of the hour by appending the word *clock* in the time readout. Do so by setting the %current_minute variable to the word *clock* if the %current_minute matches the value 00. Tasker uses the tilde (~) character to test for matching conditions, as shown in Figure 29, *Use the tilde character to test for match equality.*

We can assemble and pass the complete string to Tasker to pass to its Say function.

%current_hour %say_oh %current_minute %am_pm

Now for the moment you have been waiting for. Run the Talking Clock task by touching the run icon with the gray arrow in the lower-right corner of the Task Edit/Talking Clock screen. If everything was entered correctly, you should hear your Android device speak the correct North American current time reading to you. Awesome!

In the next section, we will embellish our Talking Clock task by having Tasker also speak at the top of every hour the current percentage of battery charge remaining. That way we will know whether we need to plug in the device for a recharge before the battery runs out of charge.

Figure 29—Use the tilde character to test for match equality.

Battery Status

Create a new Tasker task and call it Battery Status. Thanks to the fact that Tasker already has a built-in variable for current battery charge called %BATT, this new task consists of a simple step. Select the plus icon to add this step, and choose the Say action from Tasker's Misc action category. Then in the Say Text field, enter the following string:

Battery at %BATT %.

Adding the % symbol at the end of the string will make the read sound more natural (for example, "Battery at 83 percent"). Just remember to put a space between the %BATT variable and the percent symbol. Save and test the task by selecting the task's play button. Yep, all that information in just a single line of instruction. That's pretty cool, especially considering how much code this would have taken to write if this were a native Android SDK application.

The final step we need to do before assigning a profile to our Talking Clock task is to tell it to run our Battery Status task if the %current_minute value is equal to the "clock" string (remember, we set that to "clock" earlier if %current_minute matched 00). So, let's add one last step to our Talking Clock task by selecting Perform Task from the Select Task Action dialog. Save the step and run the task to hear both the current time and current battery percentage of your device. Now reopen the Perform Task step we just added and add an If condition to check whether %current_minute matches the word *clock*. Now when the clock time is at the top of the hour, the current time and remaining charge will be read out loud. The steps of the full task should look like Figure 30, *The Complete Talking Clock Tasker task*, on page 51.

There's only one more requirement to address: have the time automatically be spoken out loud every fifteen minutes during normal waking hours. To do so, we will need to create a profile for our Talking Clock task.

Creating a Profile

Now that we have our Talking Clock task defined, we need to place it into context by assigning it to a profile. Tasker profiles are triggers to run a task. These triggers can be initiated by an application running on your Android device, a starting and ending time that can also repeat at set intervals and specific days (even weeks or months). This context can also be defined by a location based on a predefined radius of GPS coordinates, the state of various apps or hardware of your device (Tasker provides more than twenty states to choose from), and events (more than forty events to choose from).

Since we want the Talking Clock task to run every fifteen minutes while we're awake, select the plus icon in the Profiles toolbar at the bottom of the screen. Name the new profile Talking Clock and select the check icon to continue. This will display a list of actions to associate the event with. Select the Time menu option as our First Context. In the Time form, set the From time a half hour before you wake up and the To time a half hour before you go to bed. In my case, that's 4:30 a.m. to 11 p.m. Check the Repeat check box and set the Talking Clock Profile option to run every fifteen minutes, as shown in Figure 31, *The Talking Clock profile settings*, on page 52.

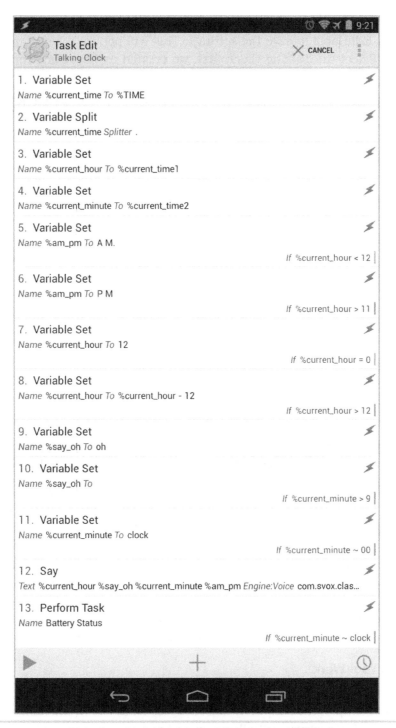

Figure 30—The Complete Talking Clock Tasker task

When you're satisfied with the start, end, and time intervals defined, select the Time Edit label to save the settings. This will pop up a list of tasks you defined. Select the Talking Clock task we created earlier. Once configured, your profile should look like Figure 32, *The Talking Clock profile*.

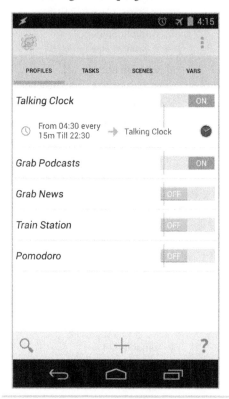

Figure 31—The Talking Clock profile settings

Figure 32—The Talking Clock profile

Now that we have instructed Tasker to run our Talking Clock profile every fifteen minutes during our waking hours, it should trigger your phone or tablet to speak the time every quarter of the hour. If it doesn't, make sure your volume is turned up and your device isn't on mute. Also, double-check your profile to make sure it is enabled. Whew! We're done!

Back Up Your Work

When you have completed any significant amount of task creation in Tasker, make a backup of the scripts by selecting the Data icon from Tasker's main menu. The Data option will allow you to back up, restore, and completely clear the tasks you have compiled in Tasker. The backup will be stored in an XML-formatted file called userbackup.xml and saved in the /sdcard/Tasker directory. As you build more Tasker profiles and tasks, copy this backup file off the device for safe keeping, just in case you need to restore the scripts or obtain a new Android device that you want to run Tasker tasks on.

As you discovered with this project, Tasker might not have the expressive scripting language of something like Ruby, but these constraints are a worthy trade-off considering the power that Tasker has to offer. Play around with the Talking Clock task by adding and subtracting steps. This will help you more quickly understand how to affect the final output. You can use what you learned in this example to create other talking alarm clock tasks, such as creating a profile that executes at 6 p.m. with a task containing a Say action reminding you that it is "Time to eat dinner."

In the next Tasker example, we will build a much simpler but very powerful task that will sound an alarm and hook that up to a profile that will trigger the task when we reach a specified geographic location. Using it, you will never fall asleep on a train or bus and accidentally miss your stop again.

4.3   Train Station Alarm

Those who regularly commute by train know all too well how the lull of a rocking train can put tired passengers to sleep in no time. If you're a light sleeper, you may hear the conductor announce your train stop. If not, you may wake up with the conductor tapping you on the shoulder and asking you to exit the train at the end of the line, usually a long way from home. If the train always runs on time, you could simply set a clock alarm to go off. But what if the train runs late because of rush-hour traffic conditions? Wouldn't it be nicer to get a few more minutes of a power nap in before confidently being alerted that you will be arriving shortly at your intended destination? Thanks to a relatively simple Tasker script, taking this idea from conception to reality will take only a few minutes to implement.

Creating the Alarm

The first thing we need to do is create a task that will sound an alarm. Do so by selecting the Task tab from Tasker's main screen and then create a new task by selecting the plus symbol in the bottom toolbar. Name the new task Alarm and then add the one and only action to this task by selecting the plus symbol in the new task screen. Since we want to sound an alert with this task, select the Alert action category. This will display the dialog shown in Figure 33, *The Select Alert Action dialog*, on page 54.

Choose the Notify Sound action and for this example name the action Train Stop Ahead. Tasker will display this name in Android's notification bar area when the action is triggered. If you prefer to display text other than the name of the task we assigned, you can do so by entering it in the Notify Sound optional Text field. Next, choose a sound file you prefer to play when this action is triggered. This can be an audio file in any format that your Android device can natively play back, such as a WAV or MP3 file. Select the file to be played back by tapping the magnifying glass icon in the Sound File row and navigating to and choosing the audio file you prefer. Once configured, your configuration should look similar to the one in Figure 34, *The Notify Sound dialog*.

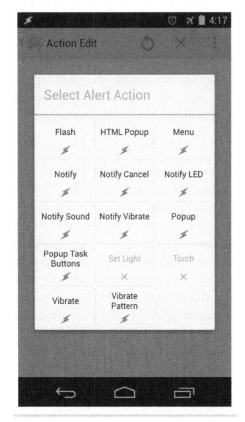

Figure 33—The Select Alert Action dialog

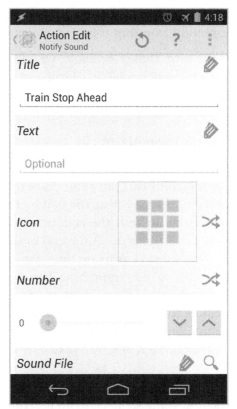

Figure 34—The Notify Sound dialog

Now that the Alarm task has been defined, we need to wrap it around a context and create a profile that will sound the alarm when a radius within a defined geographic location is entered.

Profiling the Alarm

Select Tasker's Profile tab followed by the plus symbol on the Profile toolbar. Call this new profile Train Station and choose Location from the First Context pop-up menu. A Google-powered map will appear, allowing you to place a marker at the location you want to trigger the task to run. To set the trigger marker, touch and hold the screen over the map location you want to use.

Tasker sets the default geographic radius trigger to 30 meters and sets the global GPS location sampling rate to 30 seconds. We could increase the sampling rate value located on Tasker's Monitor preference tab, as shown in Figure 22, *Network Location Check Seconds field on the Monitor tab*, on page 43, but it would also burn up our battery charge. Instead, consider how much distance a train might cover in thirty seconds and expand the trigger radius accordingly. Change this value by selecting the Radius field (this will display a list of distances in meters, as shown in Figure 35, *GPS radius list of distances*) and setting the GPS sampling radius.

In my example, I expanded this to a 300-meter radius. It's an adequate setting for my needs, since the train reduces its speed as it approaches the station. Once set, your screen will overlay a circle highlighting the event trigger area similar to the one in Figure 36, *Map with GPS radius overlay*.

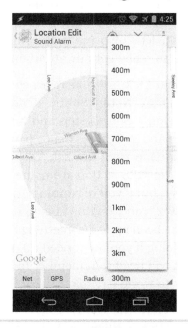 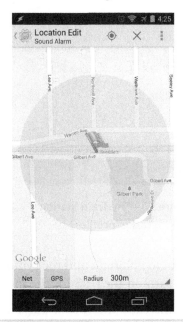

Figure 35—GPS radius list of distances   Figure 36—Map with GPS radius overlay

If you need additional time to wake up and gather your items, relocate the trigger point a quarter mile (roughly 400 meters) or further from the station. Also, expand the sampling radius to 600 or more meters depending on how fast the train is traveling. I hope that Tasker's developer allows users to enter their own radius values in a future update, since I have found that the list of radius choices can be limiting at times.

Once you have set your location marker and the desired sampling radius, touch the Location Edit label to save your settings. Tasker will then ask you to name the context that you just created. Call it Sound Alarm and assign the Alarm task we created to this context. The completed profile screen should look similar to the one shown in Figure 37, *The Train Station Tasker profile*.

Figure 37—The Train Station Tasker profile

That's all there is to it. But before placing your waking trust entirely in the alert, test the task to account for train speed, music playback volume, GPS signal, and battery consumption rate.

Enhancing the Alarm

For the alarm to work, we need to make sure the GPS radio is turned on and the music playback volume is loud enough to hear. And what the heck, let's also make the Android phone vibrate to really get our attention.

Open the Alarm task and insert a new task above the existing Notify Sound action by selecting the Notify Sound step and holding down until the Action Options dialog pops up. Select Insert Action from the list. You could try to select the GPS action from the Misc Action category, but if you're running Android OS 2.3 or newer, you won't be able to unless your device has been rooted (something I don't recommend doing if you don't need to). If you opt not to jailbreak and root your phone, you will need to remember to manually turn on the GPS for the location trigger to work.

Let's increase the media playback volume before the Notify Sound event. Select the Notify Sound step as before and select Notification Volume from the Audio Settings Action category. The default level is 3, but we'll bump that all the way up to 7, the highest level. Assuming your sound file is normalized, that sound level should definitely get your attention.

Now let's add one more activity to get our attention after the Notify Sound step. Select the plus toolbar icon in the Task Edit screen and add the Vibrate action from the Alert Action category. The default vibrate duration is 200 milliseconds. Increase that to the full 1000 milliseconds (equal to 1 second). If that isn't a long enough duration, duplicate this step for as many seconds as you need the phone to vibrate.

Test the revised profile to see how it performs, and tweak the audio levels, GPS target location, and trigger radius until you consistently and reliably set off the alarm at the time and location that works best for you. Once perfected, remember to save your work!

4.4 Tasker App Factory

The more you use Tasker, the more interesting and complex the tasks evolve to be as a result. After you build your tasks, you can share your useful and innovative scripts with others. You can export your profiles to an XML file that can be imported by other Tasker users, but what about those who have no plans on purchasing let alone learning how to use Tasker? It would be easier if you could compile your Tasker profiles into a native Android .apk application that could be distributed on the Google Play store. Thanks to a free add-on called the Tasker App Factory, you can!

Search for and install the Tasker App Factory from the Google Play market-place.[3] Once installed, the Tasker App Factory will add a new set of application compilation features into Tasker that are easy to configure and use. Let's find out just how easy it is to create an Android app using Tasker by compiling the Talking Clock task into a native TalkingClock.apk file.

Compiling Tasker Apps

Compiling and installing Tasker App Factory–generated applications requires only a few taps on the screen. In the case of the Talking Clock, go to Tasker's Task tab and touch and hold the Talking Clock task. This will add a new menu option to the top toolbar. Select this menu (it looks like three vertical dots) located in the upper-right corner. Doing so will pop up a list of options, one of which is Export. When you select the Export label, a pop-up menu will appear, as shown in Figure 38, *Task export options*, on page 58.

---

3.   https://play.google.com/store/apps/details?id=net.dinglisch.android.appfactory

Choose to export the task As App. This will display the Tasker App Factory disclaimer, essentially reminding you that Tasker's developer isn't responsible for anything bad that might happen as a result of running or distributing your program. You take full responsibility for any damage that bugs in your script, or even those of Tasker itself, might do to a user's data or device.

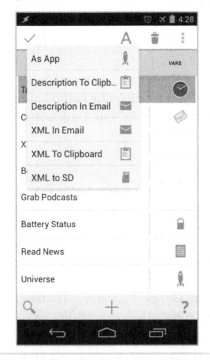

Figure 38—Task export options

Figure 39—Application package settings

After you accept the disclaimer, enter the package name (usually the namespace of your domain plus the app name), the version of the program you will build, and the name of the Tasker task you want to compile. Once completed, your configuration screen should look similar to Figure 39, *Application package settings*.

If your task requires additional permissions, such as accessing the Internet, reading contact information, writing to the file system, and the like, you will need to indicate those by selecting the Advanced Configuration check box.

Once you have completed the required configuration details, select the Configure Talking Clock label in the upper-left corner of the screen to export the task to a compiled native Android package (.apk) file. Then you can install the generated .apk directly on your device by selecting the Android robot icon located in the lower right of the Export dialog box.

Note that during the application installation process, you will most likely encounter a problem like the one shown in Figure 40, *Blocked Installation dialog* when attempting to install the .apk file on your device for the first time. This is because the Android OS by default prevents the installation of applications acquired from sources that are not directly obtained from the Google Play store.

To allow Tasker to install the freshly compiled .apk file for you, you need to give it permission to do so. This can be done by checking the "Unknown sources" option in the Security section of the Android Settings screen (Figure 41, *Allow app installations from unknown sources*).

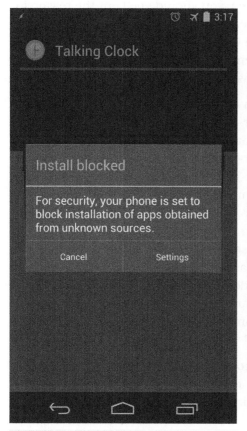

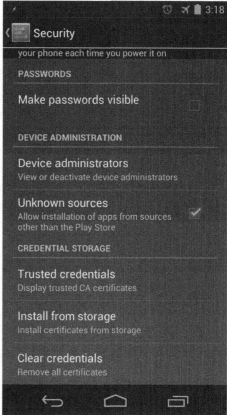

Figure 40—Blocked Installation dialog

Figure 41—Allow app installations from unknown sources

As one last security check, Android will alert you with an application display screen (Figure 42, *Talking Clock permissions alert dialog*) to remind you what permissions, if any, the application will be granted access to once it's installed.

While you already know the reasons why your compiled Tasker app needs the permissions it is asking for, others may not be aware of the data and hardware your program will have access to. If you plan on distributing your Tasker .apk files on Google Play, you had better make sure you have a good reason for requesting the permissions you need. A rule of thumb that Android users have learned over time is that any application that needs more than three sensitive-level permissions is probably an application they won't bother installing.

Figure 42—Talking Clock permissions alert dialog

If your app really needs a cornucopia of permissions, you should spell out the reason for each permission in your program's description on the Google Play market. Even then, a lot of potential users may balk at the installation permissions.

As you can imagine, the potential benefits of Tasker-compiled apps are huge. Besides that you can freely distribute or sell your own Tasker-generated native Android applications to non-Tasker users, you can also reduce the vast number of permissions required by Tasker to just those you need in your own app. In the case of the Talking Clock, there's no reason it needs to have all the permissions that Tasker needs to run. Since the Talking Clock doesn't require any special permissions, you can make the compiled Talking Clock program far more secure than the Tasker-hosted version.

Check out the Tasker App Factory Online User Guide for more information on the various options associated with the App Factory add-on.[4]

---

4.   http://tasker.dinglisch.net/userguide/en/appcreation.html

4.5 Next Steps

So, that's Tasker, the wonderfully versatile Android script and application generator that can automate a number of highly customized tasks. And you can do so without knowing anything about the Android SDK or the Java programming language. It's an amazing utility, one I use every day and one that I know you will too.

Now that you have enough of an introduction to Tasker to get started exploring on your own, here are a few ideas to jump-start your creativity:

- Run an automated daily backup of your music and photos to Dropbox or other cloud storage service while you sleep.

- Wake up to a spoken reading of your favorite RSS feeds.

- Download podcasts using your favorite podcast-catching client while you're sleeping and have the latest batch queued up and ready to go when you head out the door.

- Activate an automation Location profile when you arrive home that turns on your indoor lights and your media center and sends a text message to your family that you have arrived. For more home automation ideas using a combination of Arduino and Android programs, check out my book *Programming Your Home [Ril12]*, published by Pragmatic Bookshelf.

- Create launcher toggles to turn on and off your most frequently used hardware radios (Bluetooth, WiFi, GPS, and so on).

- Create a profile that turns off your phone's radios at the time you go to bed so you can get a good night of uninterrupted sleep.

- Capture and send a photo to your email account when the accelerometer detects movement. Add audio playback of a scream or have your device say "Put me down!" when the event is triggered.

- Detect incoming messages while driving and use the Say action to read the text so you don't have to take your eyes off the road.

- If you manage physical servers or virtual machines, ping or send HTTP requests to your machines and sound an alert if the servers fail to return a response.

- Develop your own Apple Siri or Google Now client using Tasker's Get Voice action combined with the HTTP Get action calling various web service APIs.

- Further extend Tasker's functionality to control other application events via third-party plug-ins.[5]

Visit the Tasker wiki for dozens of preconstructed Tasker profiles to give you a template to build your own Tasker scripts and applications.[6]

Next up, we'll take a look at creating Android applications and services using more traditional scripting languages like Python and Ruby. We'll also discover a couple more pleasant surprises along the way.

5. http://tasker.wikidot.com/plug-ins-and-3rd-party
6. http://tasker.wikidot.com/profile-index

CHAPTER 5

Scripting with SL4A

Utilities such as Tasker make assembling and running scripts on your Android device a breeze. Yet for those who are already fluent with a favorite scripting language, several popular choices have been ported to the Android platform. Even though many of these languages were created in an era when servers and desktop PCs were the intended hosts to run the scripts, the Android ports presented in this chapter have been retooled for the mobile experience.

While you won't be compiling most of these scripts into native Android applications, the sheer volume of code snippets and routines that have been made public for these languages is huge. And because these scripting languages are accompanied by their own libraries that handle everything from network protocols to regular expression parsing, you can accomplish a great deal of data processing with a minimal amount of code. We'll take advantage of this fact as we revisit the Talking Clock script we previously created in Tasker. We'll rewrite it in Python and Ruby with help from a host application called Scripting Layer for Android, better known as SL4A.

Because of the security model that Android enforces, applications must conform to and run within Android's Dalvik virtual machine (VM). So unless you have a rooted device and compile native system-level applications and drivers, you have to stay within the Java-centric boundaries of Android's VM.

Fortunately, there have already been a number of C-based languages like Ruby and Python that have been ported to run within the Java framework. Let's take a closer look at SL4A and the variety of languages it currently supports.

5.1 SL4A: Scripting Layer for Android

In the early days of commercial maturation of the Android OS, Googler Damon Kohler designed the SL4A to help promote the Android OS. SL4A helped differentiate Android from competitors like iOS because the early iPhone didn't allow such scripting languages to coexist on the platform. When it was first introduced, it was called the Android Scripting Environment (ASE). SL4A intended to become the host container for a variety of scripting languages. SL4A can currently host seven languages:

- BeanShell 2.0b4
- Erlang
- JRuby
- Lua 5.1.4
- PHP 5.3.3
- Perl 5.10.1
- Python 2.6.2
- Rhino 1.7R2

Unlike most of the applications and utilities featured in this book, SL4A oddly cannot be directly installed from the Google Play store. Instead, it has to be side-loaded (installed by copying the Android program to the device via a PC) or installed by downloading and installing it directly on the device. This is perplexing, since the discoverability of public Android applications is almost always made these days via a Google Play search. This is especially true for newcomers to the platform. Perhaps this is one of the reasons why SL4A continues to fly below the radar for many Android users.

You can download the sl4a_r6.apk file directly from its Google code repository.[1] Your downloaded version may be a higher number from the Release 6 I used in this book.

After the main SL4A container is installed, we will need to install both the Python and Ruby interpreters for our code examples. Launch SL4A and select View from the main menu. Then select Interpreters from the View pop-up dialog box. This will list the SL4A-compliant interpreters currently installed on your device. Select the Add icon from the Interpreters menu. A pop-up dialog will display a list of available SL4A interpreters available for download.

Installing the Python Interpreter

First choose the Python Interpreter. This downloads the PythonForAndroid_r5-2.apk package. Like the SL4A installation package, your downloaded version number may be different from the Release 5-2 I used for the examples. Install the Python package (as shown in Figure 43, *Python for Android package*, on page

---

1. https://code.google.com/p/android-scripting/downloads/

65) by opening the .apk file from your file system or via the "Download complete" label in the notification tray.

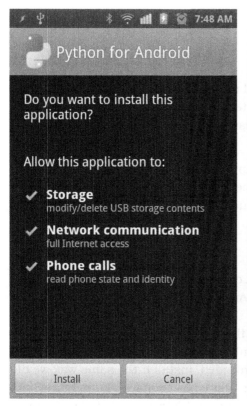

Figure 43—Python for Android package

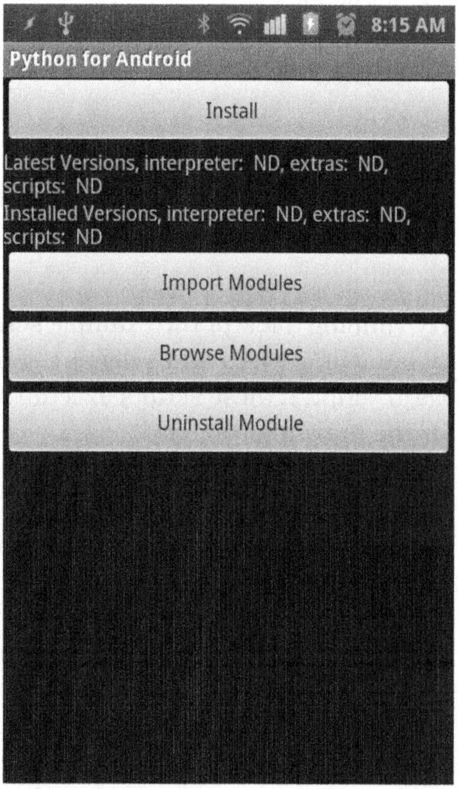

Figure 44—Python for Android interpreter and library bundles

Launch the downloaded Python installer to retrieve the interpreter files and whatever additional Python modules you need to use in your Python scripts. Do so by pressing the Install button on the screen when you load the Python for Android program, as shown in Figure 44, *Python for Android interpreter and library bundles*.

Besides the interpreter, you can also opt to install additional libraries that have been compiled to work with Python for Android. At the time I wrote this chapter, the prepackaged .egg modules freely available for download include the following:[2]

---

2. https://code.google.com/p/python/python-for-android/wiki/Modules

- pyCrypto
- PyBluez
- pyEphem
- pySerial
- Twisted
- Zope

We won't need any of these additional packages for our scripting needs, but it's pretty cool to know you can write a full-blown enterprise-class asynchronous network application and dynamic web server running on an Android phone.

Try running a few of the example scripts that came with Python for Android by launching SL4A and selecting something like the say_weather.py or take_picture.py script. If these scripts execute successfully, we're ready to do the same for the Ruby interpreter.

Installing the Ruby Interpreter

If you prefer the Ruby language, SL4A can accommodate this with the option to use the JRuby implementation on Android. Install the SL4A JRuby interpreter the same way we did earlier for the Python interpreter. From the main menu, select View, then Interpreters, then Add, and finally select the JRuby interpreter. This will initiate the download sequence and retrieve the latest JRuby for Android .apk file. Once downloaded, install it the same way we did for the Python interpreter. After the installation is complete, launch the SL4A shell application and there should be a hello_world.rb Ruby file listed in the main window. Select the file and execute the script by touching the sprocket icon. If a bounded box faded in and out from the screen (known as a *toast* message in Android-speak) and appeared with the message "Hello, Android!" then you are ready to run Ruby scripts on your Android device.

Just a quick note before we start writing some code. While the built-in SL4A editor can come in handy for quick scripts or minor edits to existing code, using it to write programs spanning more than fifty lines of code is a stretch. It's much easier to do so on a tablet paired with a Bluetooth keyboard, and it's easier still to write and test scripts on a desktop PC. Part of the reason is because of the desktop legacy these languages have inherited and partly because of the additional screen real estate available on high-resolution monitors.

But this is a temporary condition. As the rest of the world migrates to a mobile device for the majority of their computing and communication needs and as

Joe asks:
Can I Compile a Ruby Script into a Native Android Executable?

Yes, but you need a computer running Java, JRuby, the Android SDK, and a framework called Ruboto to do so.

Ruboto has two components. The first is the Ruboto gem that allows for the coding of real Android applications using a desktop computer and the Ruby syntax instead of the Java syntax. Once the aforementioned software prerequisites are satisfied, running the gem install ruboto command will install the Ruboto gem into the computer's Ruby gem collection. Then, generating a new Ruby-based Android program can be done by typing ruboto gen app --package com.mydomain.myrubyapp at the terminal of your PC. You can replace com.mydomain.myrubyapp with your domain and app name. Once the basic app template has been generated, you can use Ruby syntax to call upon the Android API for a native Android presentation experience.

The second component is called the Ruboto Core. This is the runtime library that is installed on the Android device. It is required to execute Ruboto-generated Android applications. One major benefit of installing the Ruboto Core over the standard JRuby for Android runtime is that the Ruboto Core package is installed with an Interactive Ruby Shell (IRB). It also installs a built-in editor and a cleaner user interface. This makes Ruboto Core and Ruboto IRB useful not only for developing Ruby scripts on Android but also for quickly testing Ruby code without having to resort to a desktop to see the results. You can install the Ruboto IRB from Google Play.[a] This will also prompt you to install the much larger Ruboto Core package.

If you would like to learn more about Ruboto, visit the http://ruboto.org website.

---

a.   https://play.google.com/store/apps/details?id=org.ruboto.irb

technologies like Chromecast and Miracast allow for easy broadcasting to external high-resolution monitors,[3] the day that average people exclusively use tablets for their work and play is swiftly approaching.

Now that all the dependencies have been installed and tested, we can port the Talking Clock Tasker script we created in the previous chapter to both a Python and Ruby-scripted equivalent.

5.2   Programming with SL4A

Since this is a book about Android and not about Python, Ruby, or even Java programming for that matter, I won't consume book space with language tutorials. However, the syntax for both Ruby and Python is easy enough to

---

3.   http://www.google.com/chromecast and http://www.wi-fi.org/wi-fi-certified-miracast™, respectively.

understand that you should be able to follow along. Let's begin by considering the Python port of the Talking Clock application.

Talking Clock in Python

Python programmers appreciate the fact that Python is a "batteries included" language. This means that Python already includes a good portion of functionality in its standard library. In the case of the Talking Clock script, we're going to take advantage of that fact by using Python's time library to poll the current time. We're also going to use a string-formatting function common in both Python and Ruby to help say the current time string the way we want it to be spoken. Here is the four-line Python script that speaks the current time:

SL4A/talkingclock.py
```
❶ import android
import time

❷ droid = android.Android()
❸ droid.ttsSpeak(time.strftime("The time is %_I:%M %p."))
```

Let's take a line-by-line look at what this code does:

❶ The first import statement imports the custom SL4A android library that is used to access Android-specific hardware and software functions. You will see this import statement in most Python SL4A scripts. The second statement imports Python's standard Time library, which we will use to poll and format the current time.

❷ This line initializes the android object from the Android library we imported earlier. We will use this object to pass a string value to Android's text-to-speech (TTS) parser.

❸ This line combines a few function calls. The first calls upon the time library to poll the current time. This value is passed to the strftime() function call that formats the current time into a preferred readable string. In this case, we have reformatted the current hour string to a twelve-hour clock (%_I), followed by a colon (:), followed by the current minutes (%M) and whether it's a.m. or p.m. (%p). This formatted string is then passed to the android strftime() function, where the formatted time is read by Android's default TTS engine.

You can enter this code directly into your Android device using the rudimentary text editor included in SL4A. To do so, select the Add icon from SL4A's main menu, and select Python 2.6.2 from the Add pop-up dialog. SL4A assists by giving you a head start by generating the import android statement and creating the droid object. However, as these scripts grow in length, it may be easier to either pair your phone or tablet with a Bluetooth keyboard or use a desktop computer to enter the initial code set. Then use the SL4A editor for minor tweaks and additions. Save the file as talkingclock.py via the Save & Exit icon on the SL4A toolbar.

To run the script, simply select talkingclock.py from the list of scripts on the SL4A main scripts listing. Then select the sprocket icon on the toolbar that pops up. As long as the code was typed in correctly and the volume is turned up loud enough, you should hear your Android device speak the current time. By the way, if you're interested in learning more about programming in Python, check out *Practical Programming: An Introduction to Computer Science Using Python 3 [CGMW13]* by Jennifer Campbell, Paul Gries, Jason Montojo, and Greg Wilson, available from Pragmatic Bookshelf.

Talking Clock in Ruby

Now that we have ported the Talking Clock program to Python, let's do the same thing using the Ruby language. You will see that it will be easy to program the same functionality into the script using even fewer lines of code compared to the Python version. That's because Ruby's time and date libraries are included as part of Ruby's standard language distribution, so there is no need to require more time functionality than is already there. Here's the code:

SL4A/talkingclock.rb
```
time = Time.new
droid = Android.new
droid.ttsSpeak(time.strftime("The time is %I:%M %p."))
```

That's a pretty impressive feat to be able to speak the current time in three lines of code, and it nicely shows off the power of the Ruby language.

If you're new to programming and want to learn the fundamentals using Ruby syntax, Chris Pine's book *Learn to Program [Pin09]* uses the language to teach programming essentials. If you want to delve deeper into understanding Ruby, check out Pragmatic Bookshelf's *Programming Ruby 1.9 & 2.0: The Pragmatic Programmer's Guide [TFH13]* by Dave Thomas, Chad Fowler, and Andy Hunt, which is affectionately known as the Pick-Axe book.

5.3 Scheduling the SL4A Script

Even though Tasker might not have all the tools required to code a complex parser or be able to make certain API-level calls, it has the facility to execute SL4A scripts. Using the Run Script action category,[4] you can easily hook up a timed execution of either the Python or Ruby implementation of the Talking Clock task.

---

4.   http://tasker.wikidot.com/sl4a

If you don't want to rely on Tasker to run the script at timed intervals, you could wrap either the Python or Ruby script in an infinite loop. The loop's query condition would check the current time once a minute and see whether the current minute string value is 00, 15, 30, or 45. If it is, then execute the speech event. However, this ties up the resources required to run the script, and SL4A already takes up a lot of system resources.

A third possibility would be to search the Google Play store for a utility that acts like a cron job scheduler (a Unix term for a task triggered at a predefined time). It just so happens that one exists. TaskBomb is a free (albeit ad-supported) service application that works like Tasker in that it executes applications at given times and/or time intervals.

Cron Jobs with TaskBomb

TaskBomb[5] is like a basic version of Tasker's profile feature, in that TaskBomb can be used to schedule one-off or recurring events based on time triggers. To paraphrase Ken Fehling (the application's author) regarding the description of his application, TaskBomb is basically an Android job scheduler.

By default, TaskBomb does not include built-in support for SL4A. So Ken wrote a TaskBomb add-on called the SL4A Script Launcher.[6] This extends TaskBomb to kick off SL4A scripts the same way Tasker's Run Script action works. Installing the SL4A Script Launcher from the Google Play market will add a "Select script" option to TaskBomb's Task definition Data field. With everything installed, we can build a scheduled task that will run the talking-clock.py script every fifteen minutes.

Launch the Script Launcher program and touch through the welcome and tutorial screens. If you plan on using TaskBomb beyond our simple talking clock example, take advantage of the online documentation and tutorial videos that Ken has created for the product. And if TaskBomb fulfills your needs, consider paying for the ad-free version.

Configuring a TaskBomb Task

Setting a task in TaskBomb isn't as intuitive as I would like, but once you have gone through the process the first time, it's much easier with subsequent task schedule creations. To create our Talking Clock task, we need to do the following:

---

1. Select the Tasks icon (it looks like a stick of dynamite). This will take you to the Tasks screen.

2. Select the + symbol in the upper-right corner of the Tasks screen to add a new task. This will take you to the Task definition screen.

3. Assign a name to the task (for example, Talking Clock) and, in the case of the Python version of the Talking Clock script, assign it the talkingclock.py script by selecting the Data option. This will pop up with a "Select data using" dialog. Choose the "Select script" option. This will display the files in the default SL4A scripts directory.

4. Choose the talkingclock.py script. The task has been defined. Now all we have to do is schedule it to run every fifteen minutes. To do so, return to TaskBomb's main screen and select the Schedule icon (it's the one that looks like a bundle of dynamite). Select the + icon to create a new schedule.

5. Give the name of this new schedule Talking Clock Every 15 Minutes. Next, select the Item field and assign the Talking Clock task we created earlier to the schedule. This will display the Item screen.

6. Leave the Start Time and End Time fields with their default settings, and just change the Repeat Interval field to 15 minutes. Touch the back button to save your changes.

7. The last step we need to take to get the task running is to assign the schedule a Default duration. This is how long the task will run before having to return to TaskBomb to restart the task. Since we want to run the Talking Clock task for as long as possible, set this value to 99:59:59. This will run the task every fifteen minutes for the next four days.

TaskBomb isn't the best task-scheduling software available, but it's certainly cheap and, more importantly, it works.

These simple scripting examples, combined with either Tasker or TaskBomb as the script execution triggers, only scratch the surface of what can be done. Entire legacy libraries and routines from the desktop or server can be quickly ported to run on the Android platform, making SL4A a very powerful tool on your Android utility belt.

5.4 Other Android-Ported Languages

As the hulking legacy of desktop computing continues to give way to the more nimble generation of mobile devices, developers will continue to seek out and ideally invent new languages that take into account these new platform display and resource constraints. Just as Dennis Richie invented the C language to support the shift to Unix, someone will no doubt crack the new language nut that will become the baseline upon which future programming paradigms will be constructed. In the meantime, we will contend with the advantages and disadvantages of today's popular languages during this postdesktop transition phase.

So far, we have considered only the more popular languages that can be hosted within the SL4A shell. While Perl, Python, and Ruby cover a major segment of the programming market, more ported languages are showing up in the Google Play market all the time. Here's a look at some of the more interesting additions:

- Clojure REPL[7]
- Haskell[8]
- Lisp[9]
- Scala[10] (requires root access)
- Scheme REPL[11]

As Android continues to mature, other programming languages both old and new will find their way to the platform. So, regardless of which scripting language is your favorite, tools like SL4A will be there to host them for you.

5.5 Next Steps

In this chapter, we learned about how to install and use the Scripting Layer for Android to write programs using powerful scripting languages like Python and Ruby. We also learned about scheduling those scripts to execute at predefined intervals using Tasker and TaskBomb. And we also discovered that there are a host of other programming language runtimes available for the Android platform, giving us considerable flexibility in choosing a language for building our Android scripts and applications.

Keep in mind that no matter how elegantly we structure our scripts using the approaches described in this chapter, the system resources (memory, processor utilization, and so on) consumed by interpreted scripts running on the phone are often considerably higher compared to a native Android application counterpart.

---

7. https://play.google.com/store/apps/details?id=com.sattvik.clojure_repl
8. https://play.google.com/store/apps/details?id=nl.bneijt.tryhaskell
9. https://play.google.com/store/apps/details?id=info.gomi.android.lisp.islisp
10. https://play.google.com/store/apps/details?id=com.mobilemagic.scalainstaller
11. https://play.google.com/store/apps/details?id=com.folone.replscheme

Processing for Android

All the languages I have mentioned in this chapter can interpret raw script on the fly, entirely on an Android device—no PC required. However, there are times when you may want to program a slick-looking graphically impressive native Android application without having to learn the intricacies of the Android API and OpenGL graphics programming.

Fortunately, there is an easy-to-learn language that can be used to satisfy these requirements, assuming you have access to a PC and are willing to set up the Java and Android SDK dependencies. The language is called Processing, and it may be just what you're looking for. While there currently isn't a Processing interpreter available for Android, you can use the simple syntax of the Processing language to compile a native and beautiful-looking Android application. And unlike Ruboto, there is no runtime dependency required to execute Processing-compiled apps on Android.

Processing can do more than just pretty graphics. It has access to all the major APIs, hardware sensors, radios, touch points, and just about everything else you may need to create a native Android application. Processing's syntax is also intuitive and easy to learn, allowing anyone with basic computing skills to create useful Android programs at a vastly faster rate compared to using the standard Android SDK.

To learn more about Processing for Android, read Daniel Sauter's *Rapid Android Development: Build Rich, Sensor-Based Applications with Processing [Sau12]*, published by Pragmatic Bookshelf, or visit the Processing for Android wiki page on the Processing website.[a]

---

a.   http://wiki.processing.org/w/Android

Since most of the SL4A-supported languages offer access to the Android API as well as the considerable number of libraries available for them, the potent combination of scripted access to API calls allows for some really creative uses. Here are a few ideas worthy of further exploration:

- Poll your favorite websites or Facebook or Twitter pages to verify site availability, as well as to display any new content that has been posted since you last ran the script.

- Use the camera to take a snapshot of a bar code or QR code and perform a Google lookup of the code along with a Google Images query. Pull down the results and display them in a dialog box along with price and rating details of the product in question.

- Use the respective APIs for popular web services like weather forecasts, music searches, reviewing databases, or package delivery. Poll for weather in your area based on your GPS coordinates, pull down the results, and read them to you via Android's text-to-speech engine.

• Perform a package delivery status lookup based on shipment date and tracking number. If the courier indicates that the package has been delivered, send an email or SMS containing the tracking details to the sender or other designated party.

• Submit song title and artist queries to a music search service based on a scan of your MP3 library. Return results could be everything from images of the artist to reviews of the songs or albums being searched.

• Create your own dynamic Android web server using the various web microframeworks, like Bottle and Flask for Python or Camping and Sinatra for Ruby.[12]

In the next chapter, we will put this concept into practice by creating a true, native Android SDK–based application. What's more, we will compile this application entirely on an actual Android hardware device. That's right. Unlike other mobile platforms like iOS, BlackBerry, or Windows, you can compile and deploy real, native Android applications using just your Android phone or tablet—no other computer required.

---

12. http://bottlepy.org, http://flask.pocoo.org, http://camping.io, and http://www.sinatrarb.com, respectively.

CHAPTER 6

Programming with AIDE

Up to this point, we have learned how to customize Android to look the way we want it to and to script Android to do what we want it to do. Now it's time to make Android do exactly what we want by writing and compiling a native Android application entirely on the device. This is something no other mobile operating system today has yet been capable of supporting. We will explore how to take advantage of this unique, self-contained mobile programming capability.

There are a number of benefits to using this on-device approach. First, it offers a much faster development approach compared to the more traditional tethered PC model since you don't have to go through the hassles of installing the Android SDK, the Android emulators, and the drivers necessary to transfer and debug programs compiled on the PC to the Android hardware. It's also faster because PC-based Android emulators don't emulate everything as well as the authentic hardware, such as multitouch interactions and Bluetooth, GPS, and NFC communication.

Compared to the scripting approaches we took earlier using Tasker and SL4A, native apps built with the Android software development kit (SDK) will typically consume far fewer system resources. They also often run faster than a Tasker or SL4A script because no intermediary interpreter is required to convert the scripted actions into executable code.

To demonstrate these advantages, we're going to revisit the Talking Clock program we created previously with Tasker and scripted in SL4A. We're going to take a slightly different approach compared to most introductory chapters on Android application development. Our application won't have any user interface whatsoever. And just like we did for the Tasker and SL4A versions, we will code, build, and deploy this native version of the Talking Clock program entirely on the Android device. Lastly, we will demonstrate the added benefit of native application development by enhancing the clock app with a special Android API call that isn't programmable in tools like Tasker. Let's dive in.

6.1 Getting Started

This chapter assumes you have at least some exposure to the Java language, which is the language that Android uses as its preferred development syntax. Our Talking Clock application is simple enough to understand even without much exposure to the language, but the more experience you have with Java, the better.

You will also be ahead of the class by having some familiarity with the Android SDK,[1] though this is not required. The calls that we will make to the Android APIs are not difficult to follow. The API documentation is also just a click away online for those who want to read about all the various parameters that can be passed to the functions we will be calling.

For those who would feel more comfortable learning more about the Java language before proceeding, there are numerous books, screencasts, and online resources available, and many of them are free. And for those who would like to learn more about traditional Android programming using a desktop computer, check out Pragmatic Bookshelf's *Hello, Android: Introducing Google's Mobile Development Platform [Bur10]* by Ed Burnette.

As you become more comfortable with Java and the various Android APIs, you will be able to build upon simple programs like the one presented in this chapter using more sophisticated API calls and programming logic. Like most anything else in the computing field, the more you use, the more you learn. The more you learn, the more you apply. The more you apply, the more you use.

AIDE: The Android Java IDE

So, how are we going to bring all the rich capabilities of desktop-centric Android development into the mobile constraints of an Android device? Had you asked me that question a year ago, I would have said it wasn't possible. However, a lot can happen in a year, and one of the most exciting programming tools I have seen on the Android platform to date has made this crazy dream into an entirely sane reality.

The daring developers at appfour GmbH have created AIDE—the Android Java IDE.[2] AIDE is available for download from Google Play in both a free

---

1. http://developer.android.com/sdk
2. https://play.google.com/store/apps/details?id=com.aide.ui

(albeit limited) version and a premium key (costing up to $10, though some-times on sale for much less) that unlocks all the limitations imposed by the free edition. While the limitations of the free edition won't prevent you from completing the Talking Clock project in this chapter, I recommend purchasing the premium key. Not only will it give you unrestricted file counts and add Git source code management support, doing so will also properly compensate appfour GmbH for all that hard work.

The first thing we will do is install AIDE. Then we will create a new project with it. We'll then remove some of the template-generated code we don't need and add the code we do need. Then we will compile, install, and run our Talking Clock conversion and discuss ways that we can take the project to the next level.

Creating a New Project

Download and install AIDE from the Google Play market, noting the number of permissions the app requires. appfour explains what every permission does and why, something I would like to see more Android developers who sell their wares do.

Once everything is installed, launch the AIDE app and select the "Create new App Project here..." option from the main screen. This will display an overlay that will allow you to specify the parameters to create a new application, as shown in the figure here.

Fill in the fields as shown, noting that app names cannot include spaces or special charac-ters, since this will be the name of the Android main activity Java class. As we saw earlier with the Tasker App Creator, Android apps use the package name as a unique identifier. I typically use my name (which also happens to be the name of my web domain) along with the name of the app. In my case, this is com.mikeriley.talking-clock.

Figure 45—AIDE's Create new App dialog

Leave the default App type as Hello World. Note that AIDE provides two other useful App starter templates, Tetris and Android Clock Widget. These other two project templates are definitely

AIDE Saves Time

Using the AIDE to program Android applications like the Talking Clock is a lot easier compared to the steps you would need to take if you were connecting your Android device to a desktop for development purposes. In a traditional PC desktop scenario, you would need to install the Java SDK, the Eclipse IDE, the Android SDK, and the Android Eclipse plug-in; and on Linux or Windows, you would need to configure the USB port to talk to your Android device when tethered to the computer. In addition, you would need to activate the Developer options on your Android device located in the Settings app and turn on USB debugging. That whole process often takes up a chapter in most introductory Android programming books. Developing Android programs on an Android device negates all that hassle entirely.

worth checking out on your own, but we will stick with the Hello World template. We will be making a few modifications and additions to the main class. Select the Hello World project and press the Create button. AIDE will generate all the necessary files and images required for a basic form-based Android application and open the MainActivity.java file in AIDE's code editor. The contents of this file are pretty basic.

```
package com.mikeriley.talkingclock

import android.app.*;
import android.os.*;
import android.view.*;
import android.widget.*;

public class MainActivity extends Activity
{
    /** Called when the activity is first created. */
    @Override
    public void onCreate(Bundle savedInstanceState)
    {
        super.onCreate(savedInstanceState);
        setContentView(R.layout.main);
    }
}
```

We will use this file as a starting point for our native Talking Clock project.

6.2 Programming the Clock

Before we start changing the MainActivity class, let's run the program first to ensure that AIDE has everything it needs to compile and execute the program. Select Run from the main menu, shown in Figure 46, *AIDE's main menu,* on page 79.

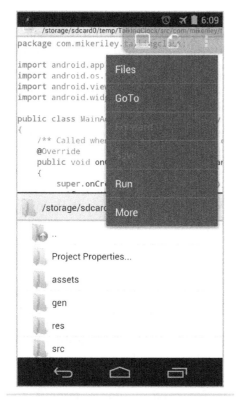

Figure 46—AIDE's main menu

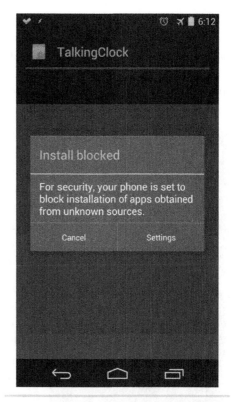

Figure 47—Block application installations from unknown sources is enabled by default on Android

This will compile the app and attempt to install it on your phone. However, as we saw with the Tasker App Creator, Android's security model prevents apps from arbitrarily installing on your device unless you give explicit permission to do so. As such, Android will display the error shown in Figure 47, *Block application installations from unknown sources is enabled by default on Android*, unless you set the security with the appropriate developer options earlier.

If this security dialog does appear, select the Settings button and check the Unknown Sources option on the Security settings screen to allow AIDE to install and execute our program. However, note that when you are not using AIDE to compile and launch applications, you should really disable the "Unknown sources security" setting. Otherwise, your Android device will be vulnerable to malicious applications installing bad things on your hardware.

With the "Unknown sources options" checked, return to AIDE and run the program again. This time, Android will ask if you want to install the application. If there are any permissions used by the app, it will list them. In the case of this application, there are no special permissions. Go ahead and select Install. When that's done, select Open. This will display the main form of the program, as shown in the following figure.

Figure 48—The MainActivity screen

Most Android applications have some kind of user interface. After all, a significant reason for the platform's success is its tactile nature of screen interface interactivity. But in our case, we're building a program that doesn't need a user interface. It just has to speak the current time and battery charge. Let's make that change.

Return to the AIDE editor and select the Main-Activity.java file from AIDE's file browser. This will open the file in AIDE's editor. Note how AIDE's code editor automatically highlights Java keyword syntax like package and import, just like a regular desktop code editor! The first thing we need to do is remove the setContentView(R.layout.main); line. If you ran the application again with this change, you would not see anything show up. That's because we removed the call to show the main layout that the boilerplate AIDE project created. We also can remove both the import android.view.*; and import android.widget.*; statements, since we won't be building a view or widget, respectively. But we do have other libraries to import.

Next we need to replace the boilerplate code that the Hello World project template generated in the MainActivity class with our own code. Once we declare a unique package name for the app so that it won't conflict with other programs on the device, we import the code libraries that we need to call the battery status on the device and perform a text-to-speech conversion of the time. Finally, we will close down any open resources and cleanly exit the program after the time is spoken.

Use a Keyboard

If you plan on typing in this code on an Android phone via the onscreen keyboard, you are far more patient than I am. Instead, you can use a paired Bluetooth keyboard or, faster yet, download the code sample from the book's website. You can also edit MainActivity.java on a desktop computer, email your phone a copy, and then paste it to the Talking Clock project directory on your Android device.

MainActivity.java

```java
package com.mikeriley.talkingclock;

import android.app.Activity;
import android.content.BroadcastReceiver;
import android.os.Bundle;
import android.content.Context;
import android.content.Intent;
import android.content.IntentFilter;
import android.speech.tts.TextToSpeech;
import android.speech.tts.TextToSpeech.OnInitListener;
import android.os.CountDownTimer;
import java.text.SimpleDateFormat;
import java.util.Date;

public class MainActivity extends Activity implements OnInitListener {

    private TextToSpeech tts;
    public String batlevel;
    public String charging;
    static final int TTS_CHECK_CODE = 0;

    private BroadcastReceiver mBatInfoReceiver = new BroadcastReceiver(){
      @Override
      public void onReceive(Context c, Intent i) {
        int level = i.getIntExtra("level", 0);
        batlevel = " at "+Integer.toString(level)+"%";

      IntentFilter ifilter = new IntentFilter(Intent.ACTION_BATTERY_CHANGED);
      Intent batteryStatus = c.registerReceiver(null, ifilter);
      int status = batteryStatus.getIntExtra(BatteryManager.EXTRA_STATUS, -1);
      boolean isCharging = status == BatteryManager.BATTERY_STATUS_CHARGING ||
                           status == BatteryManager.BATTERY_STATUS_FULL;
      if (isCharging) {
      batlevel = batlevel + " and charging.";
        }
      }
    };
```

```java
    @Override
⑥   public void onCreate(Bundle savedInstanceState) {
      super.onCreate(savedInstanceState);
      registerReceiver(mBatInfoReceiver,
        new IntentFilter(Intent.ACTION_BATTERY_CHANGED));
      tts = new TextToSpeech(this, this);
    }

    @Override
⑦   public void onInit(int status) {
      if (status == TextToSpeech.SUCCESS)
      {
        Date todaysDate = new java.util.Date();
        SimpleDateFormat hour = new SimpleDateFormat("h");
        SimpleDateFormat minute = new SimpleDateFormat("m");
        SimpleDateFormat ampm = new SimpleDateFormat("a");
        String sHour = hour.format(todaysDate);
        String sMinute = minute.format(todaysDate);
        String sAMPM = ampm.format(todaysDate);
        if (sAMPM.equals("AM")) {
          sAMPM = "A M";
        } else {
          sAMPM = "P M";
        }
        String current_hour = sHour.concat(" ");
        current_hour.replaceAll("00 ", "");
        if (sMinute.contentEquals("0")) {
          sMinute = "o clock";
        } else {
          if (sMinute.matches("\\d")) {
            sMinute = "o ".concat(sMinute);
          }
        }

        String current_time = current_hour.concat(sMinute);
        current_time = current_time.concat(sAMPM);
        String current_status = current_time.concat(batlevel);
⑧       tts.speak(current_status, TextToSpeech.QUEUE_FLUSH, null);
        new CountDownTimer(3000, 1000) {
⑨       public void onTick(long millisUntilFinished) {
        }
⑩       public void onFinish() {
          unregisterReceiver(mBatInfoReceiver);
          tts.shutdown();
          finish();
        }
      }.start();
    }
  }
}
```

❶ Here we will import all the libraries we need to call upon for the program's functions. Note that we don't need to import every class that the android.app.* and android.os.* libraries offer, just the android.app.Activity, android.os.Bundle, and android.os.CountDownTimer.

❷ To call upon the TTS engine, we have to implement the OnInitListener interface with the MainActivity class. This will also enforce declarations of the onInit(), onTick(), and onFinish() event handlers within the class, whether we use them or not.

❸ We need to create two public variables, batlevel and charging. These will hold the text string values of the current battery level and whether the battery is charging.

❹ We need to create an object called mBatInfoReceiver to collect the current battery level and assign that level to a batlevel string.

❺ Here we can determine whether the battery is currently charging. This is the bonus feature I mentioned earlier in the chapter. This is a function that we can't normally do with a standard Tasker task. We call the Battery-Manager Intent (basically an exposed routine of an application that can be called upon by another Android program) to determine whether the battery is either charging or fully charged. Either way, the battery must be connected to a power source and we pass that fact to a boolean variable called isCharging. If isCharging is true, we tack onto the batlevel string the phrase "is charging." Why would you want the device to say this when you can tell by looking if it's plugged into a power source? Consider a hands-free driving scenario, where not only knowing the time but also whether the phone was currently charging would be a nice-to-know benefit. If you're a person who is always on the go, knowing not only the time but also the battery status and charging state will help you maximize your power management. It will also remind you that your phone is tethered to a power cable and that you should disconnect it before leaving the vehicle.

❻ During the application's creation event, we register the mBatInfoReceiver so we can use it to collect the results of calling the ACTION_BATTERY_CHANGED intent. We also register the TTS engine so we can call upon it after we obtain the battery and time results.

❼ This is the heart of the program. Here we create variables to obtain the current time by calling the standard java.util.Date() Java call and then break that value down into its hour, minute, and a.m./p.m. components using a series of SimpleDateFormat objects. And just like we did in the Tasker Talking Clock script, we need to account for the twelve-hour clock, top of the hour "o'clock," and 01–09 minute "oh" designations. Then we concatenate the hour, minute, and a.m./p.m. strings together with the battery level string we obtained earlier in order to have a complete sentence to pass to the TTS engine for output.

❽ This is where we pass the compiled time and battery level string to the TTS engine to speak the output. We also need to put in a three-second CountDownTimer() to account for the reading of the string. If we don't put this delay into the program, we won't hear anything spoken because the program will exit before the speech has finished. While three seconds has worked for me, you may need to extend this to four or five seconds (4,000 or 5,000 milliseconds) if you happen to hear the end of the sentence being clipped when spoken.

❾ We don't use the onTick() event in this program, but we have to declare it to satisfy the OnInitListener implementation we used in the MainActivity class.

❿ Finally, we clean up the program by unregistering the Intent receiver we created to capture the battery level, shut down the TTS engine to free up that resource, and then call Android's finish() function to tell the OS we're done with all the variables we created. Android's garbage collector will automatically take care of the rest.

With the code out of the way, we're ready to give the project a spin!

6.3 The Clock Is Running

Just like we did earlier with the Hello World AIDE template program, run the Talking Clock project by selecting the Run option from AIDE's main menu. As long as you have allowed Unknown Sources in Android's Security settings, the application should install and give you the option to launch it. Do so by selecting the Open button. If the source code was entered correctly and the volume on your device is turned up, you should hear Android say the current time and battery level. If you have a syntax error, AIDE will let you know.

Now here's the kicker. Remember when we used Tasker to generate the Talking Clock app in the previous chapter? Well, take a look at the difference in application size of the Tasker App Factor–compiled version vs. the native AIDE-assisted one in Figure 49, *Native applications make a difference*, on page 85.

The Talking Clock program with the generic Android icon is the native program we just created, while the Tasker-generated program is the one with the clock icon that we assigned to the Tasker task and compiled in Section 4.4, *Tasker App Factory*, on page 57.

The Tasker-generated version clocks in at roughly 2MB in size. That consumes a lot of resources for such a simple program. Compare that size with the natively compiled AIDE version that comes in at a minuscule 48KB! As you may recall from the Tasker App Factory discussion, the reason for the bulky size of the Tasker App Factory–generated stand-alone applications is the runtime that must be linked into the final executable. Tasker App Factory, Mono for Android,[3] Adobe Integrated Runtime (AIR),[4] and other language abstraction tools require these bulky runtimes to execute a wide variety of application scenarios. In the case of the AIDE natively compiled app, we know exactly what the program has to do, so we have to import only the libraries we need to get the job done.

All that remains to match the scheduled functionality of the Tasker or Python and Ruby-scripted versions is the need to announce the time every fifteen minutes. The

Figure 49—Native applications make a difference.

typical approach would require us to write an Android service to run in the background, waking up every fifteen minutes to run the time and battery data collection and TTS-output routines. While writing an Android service isn't hard, it does require more intermediate knowledge of the Android SDK and Java language than we have space to cover here.

But there are alternatives we can consider. The most obvious is using Tasker's Load App task to launch our compiled Talking Clock program via a profile that runs every fifteen minutes. Of course, this goes counter to the resource-saving benefits of native apps that we just talked about. Besides, what's the point if we can just write everything we need in a Tasker script anyway?

We could also use a scheduling application like TaskBomb to kick off the app, but that's still a bit of a hassle to set up and run. And when it comes right down to it, do we really want our phone or tablet announcing the time every fifteen minutes regardless of where we're at or what we're doing? Wouldn't it

3.   http://xamarin.com/monoforandroid
4.   www.adobe.com/go/HRTDI

be better if we control the execution of this application in an appropriate setting or condition instead? That's exactly what we will do with this compiled version of the Talking Clock program.

6.4 Talking Clock Automation

Recall that in Section 3.3, *Button Control*, on page 33, we introduced Christoph Kober's Headset Button Controller application and how you can assign applications to headset button press events. In this case of the GUI-less application we just wrote, combining the Talking Clock program with Christoph's program is an ideal match.

We're going to assign the Talking Clock program with a headset button click action. I prefer using a triple-click assignment to make it more unique. When the headset button is clicked three times in a row, Headset Button Controller will launch our Talking Clock program. And because the Talking Clock app has no user interface, we don't have to worry about fiddling with a user interface while driving or walking. It's really convenient!

Compatibility Disclaimer

Note that the Headset Button Controller application works only with certain types of Android devices and headsets. For example, my Samsung Galaxy Nexus phone works perfectly with a Samsung single-button stereo headset, but my Asus Nexus 7 does not support headset buttons and therefore responds only to headset plug-in/plug-out actions.

Launch the Headset Button Controller application. Select the "Triple click" action from the Easy menu and select Launch app from "Triple click" list of options. The Headset Button Controller will then list all the applications installed on your Android device. Choose the Talking Clock application we compiled using the AIDE. Your screen should look similar to the one shown in Figure 50, *Assigning Talking Clock to a triple-click headset button action*, on page 87.

Let's do one more assignment with Headset Button Controller and run our Talking Clock application when we plug our headphones into our phone. Select the program's Advanced tab and scroll down to the "Plug in action" option within the "Headset plug in/out" category. Choose "Plug in action" followed by the "Launch app" option. Then select the Talking Clock application from the list. When you're done, your screen should look similar to Figure 51, *Assigning Talking Clock to a headset plug insertion action*, on page 87.

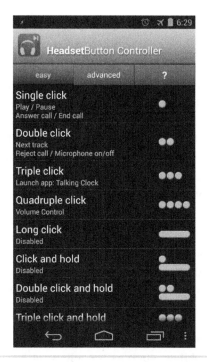

Figure 50—Assigning Talking Clock to a
triple-click headset button action

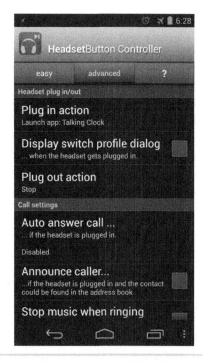

Figure 51—Assigning Talking Clock to a
headset plug insertion action

Test the assignments by plugging your headphones into your phone. You should hear the time and current battery status through your headset. If you don't, check your settings and headset volume. Once you have confirmed that the headset plug-in action works, test the triple-click assignment by triple-clicking your headset button. You should hear the same results as the plug-in test. Lastly, plug your phone into a charging cable while you have your headset attached, and triple-click the headset button. You should hear the time, the battery charge level, and the phrase "and charging" indicating that your Android phone is currently charging. Pretty sweet! As you build more native Android applications like the Talking Clock, you can expand your headset control by assigning other available headset button actions to your applications. Pretty soon you will be able to consume and react to many activities on your Android device without even looking at your screen. You could live a good portion of your mobile life with just a few clicks of a headset button.

6.5   Next Steps

In this chapter we went from zero to sixty and learned a lot about programming native Android applications. However, unlike other introductory books on Android programming, we wrote our native application entirely using the Android device. While the future of computing is clearly moving away from a desktop-centric world to a mobile-centric one, Android is the first among its competitors to declare its ecosystem entirely post PC–enabled. I suspect that Apple and Microsoft will eventually reach a milestone when developers will be able to create applications entirely on those platforms (no OS X or Windows desktop software required), but as of today, Android is in the top slot.

Now that you can build truly native Android applications without relying on an external computer or Android emulator, the speed and agility gained will allow you to rapidly prototype and build app ideas. And because these apps are built using Android's native SDK, there are no additional runtimes or dependencies required. This allows you to very quickly post your finished app online or distribute it via the Google Play store. Using the AIDE also allows you to access APIs that are not supported in third-party automation tools like Tasker. In addition to the enhanced Talking Clock application we built, consider building other short yet highly relevant utilities for your personal workflow, such as the following:

- Create a calendar event notification application using Android's Calendar Provider that goes beyond a simple audio ping alert by reading to you using Android's text-to-speech engine.[5]

- Write an integrated file transfer utility that uses Android's WiFi Direct protocol,[6] allowing you to quickly transfer files between devices without having to be connected to a WiFi access point.

- Develop a personalized messaging service app using Google Cloud Messaging for Android (GCM).[7] Although this service requires a back-end Java-based web server for message management, you could inexpensively set up this instance using Google App Engine (GAE).[8]

- Capture a series of audio notes, process them through the Google Translate API,[9] and send the output via email or SMS to a foreign language–speaking recipient.

---

5.   http://developer.android.com/guide/topics/providers/calendar-provider.html

6.   http://developer.android.com/guide/topics/connectivity/wifip2p.html

7.   http://developer.android.com/guide/google/gcm/index.html

8.   https://developers.google.com/appengine/

9.   https://developers.google.com/translate/

- Write a location-based lookup service that queries local weather, traffic, and news and that highlights your favorite store chains on a map.[10]

- Create a Near Field Communication (NFC) client that pairs with the door lock to your home or office and unlocks it with a secret code.[11]

In the next part, we will create a fully functional Android widget. But instead of relying on AIDE to build it, we're going to create the widget entirely using Tasker. By doing so, we will discover the advantages and trade-offs made between native Android application development and scripted, task-driven development.

---

10. http://developer.android.com/guide/topics/location/index.html
11. http://developer.android.com/guide/topics/connectivity/nfc/nfc.html

Part III

Build

CHAPTER 7

Tasker Pomodoro Widget

Now that we have a good introduction to using Android scripting tools like Tasker and programming tools like AIDE, let's put our knowledge to practical use by building an Android widget. As we discussed in the first part of this book, a widget is a special type of Android application that can be hosted on the Android home screen. It can autonomously update itself and run alongside other home-screen widgets.

The widget we will build is a countdown timer based on the Pomodoro Technique.[1] The basic idea behind a Pomodoro is simple—work distraction free for twenty-five minutes several times throughout a workday. There are a number of other details that go into successfully implementing the Pomodoro Technique into your own workflow, but our project widget will focus on replicating the physical kitchen clock timer that Pomodoro masters have popularized. If you're interested in learning more about the various aspects of the Pomodoro Technique, check out Staffan Nöteberg's *Pomodoro Technique Illustrated: The Easy Way to Do More in Less Time [Nö09]*, available in both print and audiobook formats.

For this project, we are going to leverage the rapid prototyping power of Tasker to help visualize the behavior of the widget. Once we have embodied the basic functionality using Tasker, fans of system optimization can consider converting the Tasker version into a native Android widget using a programming tool like the AIDE.

7.1 Rapid Tasker Prototyping

We're going to start prototyping the widget using Tasker instead of going straight for the gold and coding a native version using AIDE. That's because

---

1. http://www.pomodorotechnique.com

our end product will morph based on how we end up using the widget. Using this approach, we can quickly implement design modifications and see immediately how these changes affect the experience. This is especially important early in the development phase, where we still might not know exactly what features we want to emphasize.

If we were to modify the native Java version, we would have to go through a compile, deploy, and testing phase compared to Tasker's two-step edit-and-run process. We would also need to lug around a keyboard if we were to make a large modification to the codebase in the native client. By keeping the design iterations in Tasker for as long as possible, not only do we make the development process considerably easier on ourselves, but we also benefit from the fact that when we ultimately sit down and code the native version, we will know exactly what it needs to do.

We will begin by first outlining the basic functionality of what we want the application to do and then wire up this design in Tasker. We will encounter a few unexpected issues along the way, not apparent before we began the process, that will prompt us to make compromises in the app design as well as take advantage of the operating system. By the end of this chapter, we will have created a Tasker-based widget that fulfills a majority of our design goals.

At its core, the widget we will construct is essentially a countdown timer. We will start the countdown at twenty-five minutes by clicking the widget's icon. It will display the minutes remaining before the timer expires. When the timer reaches zero, the Android device running the widget will play a sound effect and vibrate for a brief period.

Tasker includes two types of widgets that can be hooked up to Tasker-scripted tasks. The first offers more of a shortcut to launching a task, with the main feature being the ability to control the widget's icon, related scene, and text label. The other Tasker widget offers a simple countdown timer interface that can be used to trigger a task script when the timer reaches zero. Refer to these choices in Figure 52, *Two types of Tasker widgets*.

Figure 52—Two types of
Tasker widgets

By the sound of it, using Tasker's Task Timer widget satisfies most of our application's requirements. Yet before we jump to placing this Tasker widget on the home screen, we first need to construct the task that the widget will run when the countdown is finished.

First Task

When the timer expires, we want to hear an audio cue and feel the phone vibrate, so let's build a task to do just that. Open Tasker and select the Tasks tab. Create a new task by selecting the plus icon. Call the task Pomodoro in the New Task textbox that pops up. Select the check icon to accept the name and proceed to the task definition dialog. Add a task that plays a sound. We will eventually have Tasker play a custom sound of our choice, but in the interest of saving time in this initial design pass, select an existing ring tone for the audio cue.

Next, select the plus icon in the lower toolbar to add a new task, and choose the "Media action" category. From there, choose the Play Ringtone action. Select your ring tone of choice by touching the magnifying glass icon to the right of the Sound property. This will display a list of all the ring tones available on your phone. You can play back this sound via Android's six sound channels by selecting the list of Stream options. Let's leave it on the default Notification channel. Touch the Action Edit label in the upper-left corner of the form to save this first step in the Pomodoro task.

Now let's add the Vibrate step. Select the plus icon to add a second step to the Pomodoro task, and choose the "Alert action" category. Then select Vibrate from the grid of alert actions. The default duration of the Vibrate function is 200 milliseconds. This brief burst may be too short to notice, so let's triple this vibration time to 600 milliseconds.

Finally, let's assign a built-in icon to the task so that when it appears on the home page in its widget trigger form, it looks more appropriate than Tasker's default sprocket icon. Select the Image Select icon on the far lower-right corner of the Pomodoro task dialog. It looks like a gray checkerboard. By selecting this icon, the Image Select pop-up will appear, allowing you to choose the source of your icon. Select Built-In Icon. This will display a variety of icons that are available to all Tasker profiles and tasks. One of those built-in icons is a clock. Choose that, and Tasker will show that icon when the widget associated with that task is displayed on the home page. If everything went according to plan, your Pomodoro task should look like Figure 53, *The Pomodoro task in Tasker*, on page 96.

With our task defined, we can now assign it to the Tasker countdown widget.

Countdown Widget

Return to Android's home screen and select the Task Timer Tasker widget from the Android Widget screen or via the selection dialog that pops up when you press and hold your finger on the home screen. Place the Task Timer widget on an open area on your home screen and assign the Pomodoro task we just created to the timer. Before accepting the selection, press the timer clock in the lower-right corner of the Widget/Pomodoro dialog that appears and set the Minutes field to 25. Select the green check to approve the settings. This will place the timer on your home screen and preset the clock timer to twenty-five minutes, ready for action. The home page widget should look similar to Figure 54, *Setting the Pomodoro Timer widget.*

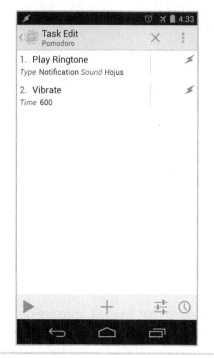

Figure 53—The Pomodoro task in Tasker

Figure 54—Setting the Pomodoro Timer widget

Test the Timer

Before we start the timer, let's first make sure the ring tone and vibration duration adequately meets our requirements. Open the Pomodoro task in Tasker and select the gray Play icon in the lower-left corner of the Task Edit

Pomodoro dialog. If the ring tone isn't loud enough or the vibration isn't long enough, tweak those settings until they work best for you. Then return to the home screen where you placed the Task Timer widget and select the clock icon associated with it. This will display a large timer dialog with Days, Hours, Mins, and Secs preset for twenty-five minutes based on our earlier starting timer value assignment. Select the OK button in the lower-right corner of the dialog to start the countdown.

The timer readout text on the widget will turn green, indicating that the countdown clock is running. You can pause the countdown by tapping this green text readout, upon which the timer text will change from green to red. Tapping the text again will start the countdown again where it left off. To reset the timer, tap the clock icon we assigned the task to once again pop up the timer dialog. The timer value will return to its original default of twenty-five minutes. You can also change the value here as well, such as setting it for two minutes to test the task trigger vs. waiting a full twenty-five minutes. Select the green check icon to proceed with the countdown. When the Task Timer widget text reads 00 00 00 00, the Pomodoro task we created should kick off, playing the assigned ring tone and vibrating the phone for a little more than half a second.

If your Android device has an aggressive power management setting, it might shut off the phone and prevent the timer from counting down and triggering the Pomodoro task. This is because Android by default doesn't want widgets to continue running while the device is in standby mode. You can imagine the impact a dozen widgets polling the network or constantly refreshing graphics to the screen would have on battery charge and system performance. Unless an application or widget specifically requires wake lock in its manifest of permissions, the Android OS will take over and do its job. In the case of Tasker, it was already granted this permission (not to mention a bunch of other system-wide permissions) when you installed it.

So, if the timer behaves erratically, force the task to keep your Android device awake by editing the Pomodoro task in Tasker and selecting the Task Properties icon to the right of the clock icon we assigned earlier in the Task Edit dialog. Then check the Keep Device Awake box and heed the warning that Tasker reminds you about battery drain when selecting this option for resource-intensive tasks.

Task Timer Limitations

Well, that was pretty easy. In fact, once you become proficient with Tasker, you should be able to rebuild this simple countdown timer widget in less than a minute. Considering the time it would take to construct a comparable native widget from scratch, that's pretty amazing and further helps showcase Tasker's power and versatility. If you're satisfied with the timer, then we're done! There's no need to read the rest of this chapter. But if you're like me, you want the widget to do more.

How about playing a wind-up sound that emulates a real kitchen clock timer and sounds a ding from that same kind of timer at the end of the Pomodoro? Wouldn't it also be nice for the Android network radio to turn off so we aren't interrupted with email notifications and Twitter tweets and turn back on when the Pomodoro session has finished? To add these and other enhancements, we need to take a different approach to our widget construction. Let's proceed to do just that.

7.2 Pomodoro Widget Redux

Our first attempt at a Pomodoro widget went pretty well, considering how little effort was required to build it. Now it's time to step up our game and add more features and polish to the widget.

One of those enhancements is the elimination of the unnecessary days, hours, and seconds field from the Task Timer widget, since we are primarily interested in minutes remaining in the countdown. Unfortunately, the Task Timer widget currently does not allow hiding of these fields. We will have to think differently.

Widget Requirements, Take Two

Let's take what we have already assembled and build upon the basic premise of a countdown timer with an audible alarm. Then let's consider the other things we would like this widget to do for us.

1. Before the countdown begins, play an audio clip of a kitchen clock timer being wound up.

2. Turn off the cellular and WiFi radios so we can minimize disruptions for the duration of the Pomodoro.

3. Display only minutes remaining in the countdown on the widget.

4. When the countdown reaches zero, display the phrase "DONE!" in the widget's label area, play an audio clip of a kitchen clock timer's ding sound, and vibrate the device.

5. When the Pomodoro is done, stop the task and turn the cellular and WiFi radios back on.

We could add other tasks as well with the start and stop events of the Pomodoro, but these should give us enough to work with for now. But because of the way the Task Timer widget works and displays the countdown clock, we're going to have to ditch it in favor of Tasker's other widget, simply called the Task widget.

Creating the Tasks

The fact that our revised widget design needs to be completely self-contained presents us with a conundrum. How do we host both a start action (by touching the widget) and a stop action (when the timer runs out) in a single widget? While we might be able to devise a convoluted if-then statement structure in a single task, a more elegant approach that we will employ is creating two tasks. One will be used to trigger the start of the countdown, and the other will be responsible for incrementing the countdown clock and doing something when the time runs out. We will start with building the task that will start the clock.

Choosing an Audio Clip

Based on our requirements, we need to play the sound of a kitchen timer being wound up. You could scour the Web for sound effects or record your own with your Android device. The easiest option would be to download the pomostart.mp3 file from this book's code download page on the Pragmatic Bookshelf website. This file, along with the audio file pomostop.mp3, were generously provided by Andy Hunt, Pragmatic Bookshelf publisher and audio engineer extraordinaire. Andy was the recording engineer for Pragmatic Bookshelf's first audiobook, which just happened to be the audio version of Staffan Nöteberg's *Pomodoro Technique Illustrated: The Easy Way to Do More in Less Time [Nö09]*.

Note that while these audio files can be freely downloaded as part of this book's source code bundle from the Pragmatic Bookshelf website and used in your own applications, please be kind and attribute Andy's work if you use the audio clips in any applications that you distribute. Free is nice, and being courteous about it is nicer!

Once you have obtained an MP3 audio start clip of your choice (for the purposes of this exercise, I'll assume you chose the pomostart.mp3 file), copy the file to the Ringtones folder on your Android device. You can do this either by downloading the file from the Web and saving it directly in the /sdcard/Ringtones folder or by mounting Android's file system on your computer and copying it via either File Explorer on Windows or the Android File Transfer program for OS X.[2] You might as well save some time and copy the sound clip for when

---

2. http://www.android.com/filetransfer/

the timer countdown expires, and I'll assume you chose the pomostop.mp3 file available from this book's code download bundle.

With both MP3 audio clips now stored in the /sdcard/Ringtones folder, launch Tasker and create a new task called PomoStart. Then create a step that plays the pomostart.mp3 audio file. Do so by selecting the plus icon in the lower toolbar of the Task Edit dialog. Then select the Media category followed by the Music Play option. With the Music Play screen displayed, select the magnifying glass icon to the right of the File label and navigate the File Select dialog to the Ringtones folder. Then choose the pomostart.mp3 file. Upon doing so, the screen should look like the figure shown here.

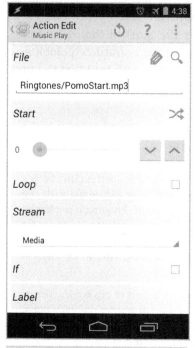

Figure 55—The Music Play task dialog

Leave the Stream option set to Media. This will play back the MP3 audio clip on the same channel and volume as the standard Android audio application (such as the music player) volume. After accepting the settings by choosing the Action Edit label in the upper-left corner of the dialog, verify that Tasker can correctly locate and play back the file and that the volume is loud enough to hear. Do this by selecting the Play icon in the lower-right corner of the PomoStart task edit dialog. If you don't hear anything, check your Android's volume and mute settings. If successful, you should hear a few windings of a kitchen clock timer.

Turn Off the Radios

The next item on the requirements agenda to tackle is disabling the WiFi and 3G radios so that we are not distracted by incoming emails, Twitter, and other social network notifications. Tasker can granularly turn off some of Android's radios. In Android OS versions prior to 4.2, Tasker and other applications could programmatically turn on and off airplane mode, thereby disabling all radios in an instant. Version 4.2 no longer allows this autonomous activity except in the unlikely state that your application has root-level access.

\]/
~f
Joe asks:
Why Can't I Automatically Turn On and Off Android's Airplane Mode or GPS Radio?

Prior to Android 4.2 (aka Jelly Bean), you could enable and disable Android's airplane mode or GPS radio from an Android application or Tasker task. Beginning with the release of Jelly Bean, Google smartly decided that it wasn't a good idea to give applications the ability to turn on and off Android's cellular and GPS radios. For example, consider a scenario of traveling overseas where cellular data rates are exorbitantly expensive. You explicitly turn on airplane mode to block the phone from connecting to the cell towers to exchange data.

Thinking that all is well, you discover midway through your trip that a demanding application decided to override your settings and forcibly disable airplane mode and allow your device's cellular radio to chatter away. Worse yet, a malicious application could decide to upload your screen activity captured from the previous day at 3 a.m. when you're likely asleep. You would expect to have the airplane mode protect your device from these scenarios, and it would be quite an angry disappointment if the phone took instructions from something other than you for such a critically important setting.

If you still have a burning desire to activate and deactivate the airplane mode or GPS radio within a Tasker task, you can do so by jailbreaking and rooting your Android device. Doing so will not only provide Tasker with the elevated system privileges of turning on and off airplane mode but also grant control to a number of other system-level functions, including forcing the display to stay on regardless of power settings, putting the WiFi radio to sleep, and rebooting the phone.

Add the WiFi Off action to the PomoStart task by selecting the plus icon, and select the "Net action" category. When the Net Action Category dialog is displayed, choose the WiFi action and leave the default value set to Off. Do the same thing for the Mobile Data action by choosing the plus icon to add a new action. Select the Net action category and then the Mobile Data option. Like the WiFi action, set the Mobile Data option to Off.

Return to the PomoStart task edit dialog. Before trying the expanded task, check to see whether your WiFi and Mobile radios are turned on. Return to the PomoStart task edit dialog and select the play icon to run the task. After the clock winding sounds, your mobile and WiFi radios should turn off. Verify this by opening Android's web browser and attempt to load your favorite website. The browser should complain that the web page you were trying to reach is unavailable.

Start the Countdown

So, we're done with starting up the Pomodoro Widget clock, right? Not quite. We still need an action in this task to initialize the starting countdown value and then trigger the countdown activity. Let's go through this process step by step:

1. Create a new action in the PomoStart task via the task's plus icon and select Variable from the Select Action Category dialog. Then choose the Variable Set action. Create a new global variable name called %COUNTDOWN and set its initial value to 25 to represent the duration of the Pomodoro. Now that we have initialized the clock to twenty-five minutes, we need to actually start the countdown. But we won't be able to do that until we define a second task that manages the clock countdown behavior. Let's do that next.

2. Create a new task and call it PomoWidget. This is going to be the task that is run when PomoStart calls on it to start running. After that, we need to decrement the value of the %COUNTDOWN variable each time the PomoWidget task is called. How do we run the PomoWidget task at a fixed, repeating time duration? We will need to create a time-based profile that triggers the PomoWidget task to run. But before we do that, we first need to define a few more actions in the PomoWidget task.

Besides getting the PomoWidget task to run at a set interval, we also need to stop the countdown once it reaches zero, play back the pomostop.mp3 audio clip, vibrate our Android device, and turn the WiFi and Mobile Data radios back on. Let's work backward and address the latter requirements first.

We already know how to turn on and off the WiFi and Mobile Data radios from the PomoStart task, so let's repeat those actions in the PomoWidget task with one small addition. Select the add action plus icon and then the Net action category followed by the WiFi action. Set the WiFi option to On. Since we don't want the WiFi radio to turn on until the timer reaches zero, also select the If check box in the WiFi action dialog to check whether %COUNTDOWN is less than the value of 1. Once set, the WiFi action dialog should look like Figure 56, *Set WiFi On Action dialog*, on page 103.

Save the changes and repeat these same steps for the Mobile Data action. And just as we set the PomoStart task to play back the pomostart.mp3 audio file, we will do the same by assigning a new action to play the pomostop.mp3 file.

1. Create a new action in the PomoWidget task, and select the "Media action" category followed by the Music Play action. When the Music Play action dialog appears, select the magnifying glass icon to select the MP3 file located at Ringtones/pomostop.mp3. We also need to check the If box to check and see whether the condition of the %COUNTDOWN variable is less than 1, since we don't want the kitchen clock ding to sound until the timer runs out.

Figure 56—Set WiFi On Action dialog

2. We can also set the Vibrate action using the same approach as the radio activation and sound file playback steps. Namely, create a new action in the PomoWidget task and select the "Alert action" category followed by the Vibrate action. Set the time to 600 milliseconds. You can set the vibrate duration longer if you prefer, but I find that 600 milliseconds is just right for my needs.

3. We also need to check the value of the %COUNTDOWN variable so as not to trigger the Vibrate action until our timer reaches zero, so check the If box in the Vibrate dialog and test for the condition If %COUNTDOWN < 1. Upon saving this action step, you should now have actions that play the pomostop.mp3 audio clip, turn the Mobile Data and WiFi radios back on, and vibrate the device for slightly more than half a second.

4. One more action we need to add to the PomoWidget task is decrementing the %COUNTDOWN variable so that each time the task is run, we reduce the countdown by one. So, add a Variable Set action that sets the %COUNTDOWN variable equal to %COUNTDOWN minus 1. We need to do this as long as %COUNTDOWN is greater than zero since we don't want to take our countdown into negative number territory. So, in this Variable Set action step, check the If box to test If %COUNTDOWN > 0 and save the action and the PomoWidget task.

Good work! But we still have a few more things to take care of, namely, setting the Pomodoro task to execute at set intervals as well as show the remaining countdown value in the icon text area of the Tasker-generated Pomodoro widget that we will create on our home screen.

Pomodoro Profile

To decrement the countdown value to eventually reach zero, we will create a Tasker profile to run the PomoWidget task at a set timed interval. Create a new profile by clicking the plus icon in Tasker's Profile tab and call the new profile Pomodoro.

When the First Context dialog pops up, select the Time option since we want to run the PomoWidget task at a timed interval. In the screen that follows, deselect the check marks for the From and To ranges and then select the Repeat check box. Then set the repeat value to run the task every one minute and select the green check icon in the lower-left corner of the dialog to accept the value. But there's a problem. Tasker won't accept our value of running the task every one minute, as you can see in the following figure.

Figure 57—Tasker will not execute profiles at an interval less than two minutes apart.

It looks like Tasker won't let us set up a profile to run a task at intervals less than two minutes apart. The reason for this limitation is to prevent the task(s) assigned to a profile from running so frequently as to have a notable degrading impact on your Android's battery charge. So, in order for us to create this Pomodoro timed interval context, we have no choice but to set the lowest value of the context interval to execute every two minutes.

Now that we have created the timed interval context, we need to assign it to a task. From the Task Selection dialog that popped up after we accepted the context interval, select the PomoWidget task we created earlier. We now have a Pomodoro context to trigger our PomoWidget task every two minutes. Cool! With a context ready to run our PomoWidget countdown task every two minutes, we can create the widget, right? Not yet. We still have a few more important issues to address. The first is figuring out how to set the Pomodoro timed interval context to start running when we touch the Pomodoro widget icon. We also have to find a way to stop running the context when the countdown reaches zero. Lastly, it would be good user feedback to see the current value of %COUNTDOWN on the widget's icon text field so we know how much time is remaining before the countdown clock expires.

1. To address starting the Pomodoro context upon the touch of the widget icon, we can call upon a helpful task action in Tasker called Profile Status. Open the PomoStart task for editing and add a task. Select the Tasker action category, followed by the Profile Status action. Name the Profile Status action Pomodoro and set the task to On. This means that when the PomoStart task is run, it will turn on the normally disabled Pomodoro profile containing the instruction to run the PomoWidget action every two minutes.

2. We have a running clock, but now we have to instruct the profile to turn off when %COUNTDOWN reaches zero. To do so, open the PomoWidget task for editing and add a Profile Status action called Pomodoro, just like we did for the PomoStart task. But this time, instead of setting the value to On, we are going to set Profile Status to Off under one condition, that being If %COUNTDOWN < 1. When set correctly, the Profile Status dialog for this task should look like the figure here.

Figure 58—Turning off the Pomodoro profile when the countdown ends

Time Remaining

With the starting and stopping actions of the Pomodoro profile interval timer in place, we're almost ready to test our widget. But before we do, we still need to display the remaining time on the widget. It would also be a nice touch if we displayed "DONE!" in addition to the other concluding tasks we set up earlier (turning the radios back on, playing the pomostop.mp3 audio file, and so on). The "DONE!" label will also come in handy when testing for the first time you touch the widget to start the clock.

1. Open the PomoWidget task for editing and add a Variable Set action via the plus icon; then select the Variable Action category and then the Variable Set action. In the Name field, enter the %COUNTDOWN variable we've been tracking all this time. But instead of setting it to a number, we are

going to set it to DONE! as long as the condition If %COUNTDOWN < 1 is true. Set the If statement accordingly and save the action.

2. At last, we need to add an action to the PomoWidget task that displays the current value of %COUNTDOWN on the widget icon text. Do so by selecting the plus icon while editing the PomoWidget task and choose the Tasker Action category. From there, select the Set Widget Label action. Call the action PomoWidget and set its label to %COUNTDOWN. By doing so, the current value of the %COUNTDOWN variable will be displayed and updated each time the PomoWidget task is run.

Finishing Touches

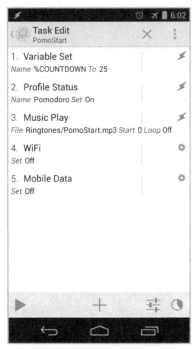

Figure 59—The PomoStart task

Let's do one more thing and place the proverbial cherry on top of our creation. Let's assign an icon to the PomoWidget task so that when we place the Tasker widget on our home screen and assign it to the PomoWidget task, Tasker knows to use the icon we assigned the PomoWidget task rather than Tasker's default sprocket icon. Assign the icon by opening the PomoWidget task for editing and selecting the checkerboard icon in the lower-right corner. This will display the Image Select dialog. You can assign whatever image you like for the icon. These include existing application icons, bundled icons installed with Tasker, and individual icon files. Icon sets for Tasker can also be downloaded from the Play app store or obtained from commercial websites like Iconfinder.[3]

With all the pieces now in place, your PomoStart and PomoWidget tasks should look like the screens in Figure 59, *The PomoStart task*, and Figure 60, *The PomoWidget task*, on page 107, respectively, and the Pomodoro profile should look like the one shown in Figure 61, *The final Pomodoro profile*, on page 107.

Verify that these screens look similar to yours, making sure to account for the %COUNTDOWN variable assignments and conditional tests in the right order.

---

3. http://www.iconfinder.com

Figure 60—The PomoWidget task

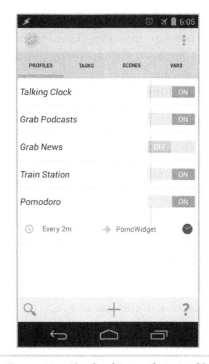

Figure 61—The final Pomodoro profile

The big moment has finally arrived. It's time to try our Tasker-constructed Pomodoro widget and see whether it performs the way we expect it to perform.

7.3 Testing the Revised Widget

Tasker lacks any type of traditional programming debugging tools. As such, we have to rely on old-fashioned brute-force testing of running the script over and over again until it produces the desired response. In the case of our widget, we need to set up the onscreen widget, initiate the countdown, observe the results, and modify until the intended outcome is achieved. We will begin by hooking up the tasks we wrote to a home-screen widget.

Creating our widget on the home screen is similar to the way we did it earlier. But this time, instead of selecting Tasker's Task Timer widget, we're going to choose Tasker's Task widget. Upon doing so, Tasker's Task Selection dialog will pop up onscreen. Locate and select the PomoWidget task. Tasker will then display the PomoWidget task in case we want to do any further editing before we accept the placement of the widget. Since we don't have any additional editing to do at the moment, select the check mark to set the widget on the home page. Note that the initial icon text of the widget partially displays the PomoWidget label.

If you don't disturb the widget, you will eventually notice that the label will refresh and show the number 25. Two minutes later, it should read 23, and so on. Or at least that's what is supposed to happen. But that's not what is happening. Instead of decrementing the countdown by two units every two minutes, it is decrementing the number by only one. Why is this happening?

Remember when we set up the task to decrement %COUNTDOWN by 1 each time the PomoWidget task was run? Well, that would have worked had Tasker allowed us to run the task once a minute. But Tasker restricts us to running tasks at a minimum of every two minutes. That means we need to change the Variable Set action in the PomoWidget task from %COUNTDOWN - 1 to %COUNTDOWN - 2. Go ahead and do that now and save the changes to the PomoWidget task. Note that you don't have to remove the widget you just created. Instead, just edit the PomoWidget task in Tasker, and the widget we created earlier will simply adopt the new instructions. That's pretty cool.

Return to the home screen where you placed the PomoWidget task-assigned widget. Now repeatedly touch the widget to more quickly advance the countdown. Observe that with each touch, the countdown value will decrement the displayed countdown value by 2. The reason for this behavior is because when you touch the widget, you are executing the PomoWidget task again. Doing so decrements the %COUNTDOWN variable accordingly.

Keep touching the widget until it displays the "DONE!" label. When "DONE!" finally shows up, you should also hear the Ding! audio clip, feel the device vibrate (if it's an Android phone, since Android tablets usually don't have a vibrate function because they don't usually fit in a pocket), and see your WiFi and mobile radios turn back on. While you could have just let the Pomodoro Tasker profile execute the PomoWidget task every two minutes, touching the widget to execute the PomoWidget task allows us to more quickly test the start and stop actions.

Now let's start the timer again from the beginning. Touch the widget and take notice of the starting time. You should have heard the winding clock audio clip play and seen the WiFi and mobile radios turn off. But something still isn't quite right. The widget icon text shows a starting value of 23. If you practice the Pomodoro Technique, Pomodoro durations are supposed to last for twenty-five minutes, not twenty-three minutes. We have another bug, and just like the last bug we fixed, this one is just as easy to spot and fix. Remember when we set the starting value of %COUNTDOWN equal to 25 in the PomoStart task? Well, that value didn't take into account that PomoWidget runs each time we touch the widget.

Since we have to touch the widget to start the clock, the PomoWidget task ran and immediately decremented our starting value of 25 to 23, even though two minutes didn't pass yet. So, to fix this, simply edit the Variable Set action in the PomoStart task and change the %COUNTDOWN variable from 25 to 27 so that it looks like Figure 62, *Starting %COUNTDOWN at 27 instead of 25.*

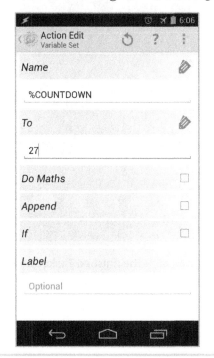

Figure 62—Starting %COUNTDOWN at 27 instead of 25

Figure 63—The final PomoStart task

With these two bugs eradicated, the PomoStart and PomoWidget tasks should now look like the ones shown in Figure 63, *The final PomoStart task*, and Figure 64, *The final PomoWidget task*, on page 110, respectively.

Head back to the home screen and repeatedly touch the widget until it decrements to showing the "DONE!" label. Wait for the ending Ding! audio clip to play and the radios to turn back on. Then touch the widget again to restart the timer. If the changes were made correctly, you should see the icon text display a starting value of 25 and properly decrement by two every two minutes. When the countdown expires, the icon text will show "DONE!" and you should hear the concluding Ding! audio effect, feel the vibration, and notice the radios turn back on.

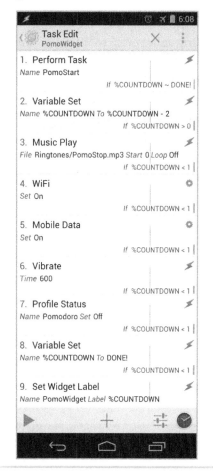

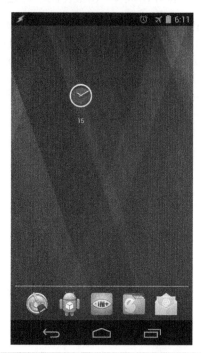

Figure 65—The finished Tasker-built Pomodoro widget

Figure 64—The final PomoWidget task

Once you have confirmed that everything is working as expected, you can take advantage of Android's widget behaviors and move the Pomodoro widget to any screen location that works for your layout needs. I prefer a dedicated uncluttered screen for mine (as shown in Figure 65, *The finished Tasker-built*

Pomodoro widget) so that I'm not distracted by any other widgets while working through my Pomodoro sessions.

Congratulations! You just built a very slick and especially handy Pomodoro widget for your Android device. You also saved yourself a little money in the process, since you no longer need to purchase one of several Pomodoro widgets available in the Google Play market.

7.4 Addressing the Limitations

Creating the Pomodoro widget entirely in Tasker is a nice showcase of how powerful Tasker is for building your own widgets. But it also shows off Tasker's limitations. A couple of problems with the widget's current implementation are as follows:

* The icon text label updates only every two minutes because of Tasker's two-minute profile execution limitation. It would be more intuitive to see the time remaining reflected every minute, just as you would expect a countdown to behave.

* When the countdown is finished and the remaining time is replaced by the "DONE!" label, the "DONE!" label persists until the next time the widget is touched again so that the countdown can be reinitiated. It would be nicer to see the "DONE!" label replaced with something like Pomodoro when the widget is not in use. Fixing this in Tasker isn't difficult. You would essentially need to set up a PomoStop task coupled with a profile that fires after a certain duration has passed after the Pomodoro countdown has finished. But it would be nicer if such a growing list of tasks and profiles could all be self-contained in a single package such as a native Android widget.

* The widget is susceptible to advancing the time when it is touched. While this so-called feature was helpful during the testing of our widget, it's probably not necessary (and perhaps even undesirable) in working production mode. A more intuitive behavior would be to touch the widget to start and stop the countdown and perhaps use a double-tap or a long-press to restart the countdown and/or bring up a dialog that allowed us to modify the countdown time.

* Speaking of modifying the countdown duration, customizing the time requires us to open the PomoStart task in Tasker and edit the initial Variable Set value for %COUNTDOWN each time we want to set the duration to something other than twenty-five minutes. Granted, true practitioners of the Pomodoro Technique shouldn't deviate from the twenty-five minute

duration, but some individuals would likely appreciate the ability to easily modify the duration for their own time-boxing practices. While you could build a dialog box using Tasker's scenes capability that allowed users to modify the duration in a graphical way rather than directly editing the PomoStart task, doing so would require time to learn how to use scenes as well as to build the dialog and the task structure to support it. Again, that time would probably be better spent investing in building a native widget instead.

- Distributing this widget to other Android users who don't own Tasker isn't possible, since the current version of Tasker App Factory does not support widget generation (although Tasker's developer has hinted that this may be possible in a future release). Therefore, only those who have already bought and are actively using Tasker can use this Pomodoro widget prototype. Even if you sent these Tasker users the task list, they would still need to wire up the profile and widget on their own. Considering we spent a chunk of this chapter on that very subject, asking others to set up this widget is nowhere near as intuitive as downloading and installing a widget from the Google Play store.

- Most important is the fact that our Tasker-based Pomodoro widget is not a real widget in the truest sense of the Android ecosystem. Yes, Tasker's own Task and Task Timer widgets are real widgets, but the Tasker Task widget is simply a wrapper that needs to point to a task written in Tasker to use. We can't see our Tasker-based Pomodoro widget on Android's widget selection screen (along with a nice graphic indicating the widget itself), and it can't be resized like some other native Android widgets allow.

While some of these issues could be addressed in Tasker, the amount of time and effort to do so would probably be better spent investing in programming a native Pomodoro widget. But using a programming tool like the AIDE makes this a possibility. AIDE even has a widget project template you can use to get started. Those interested in taking Tasker widgets to the next level should further explore the AIDE. You can use AIDE to code enhancements that would be difficult if not impossible to do using Tasker alone.

Even with the option to pursue a native development path, Tasker has certainly served its purpose by helping us envision and bring to life a working Pomodoro widget. It has also allowed us to create this working widget in considerably less time than it would take to develop a native Android widget that does more or less the same thing.

7.5 Next Steps

We spent quite a bit of time going over the construction of the Pomodoro widget using Tasker. But now that you know the specifics of doing so, building a Tasker widget from scratch should be a much faster and more intuitive experience. This chapter also introduced a number of new ideas and Tasker features, including audio playback and event intervals, that you will be able to apply to other Tasker-related projects. You can also use the Pomodoro widget as a foundation to build other interval-driven task triggers. We can also enhance the widget with features that will deliver more than just a Pomodoro stop clock. Here are a couple of ideas to get you started:

- Make a call to the Talking Clock Tasker project when the countdown ends so you will know the current time without having to look at your phone or tablet.

- Write the date and timestamp of the Pomodoros you practice to a text file using Tasker's Write File action. Create a Tasker scene to view the data, send it as an email attachment, or post it to a website.

- If you enjoy listening to music but want to make sure the music stops during the Pomodoro and starts back up again after the Pomodoro period is completed, call upon Tasker's Music Stop and Music Start Media actions, respectively.

- Reward yourself with the successful completion of a Pomodoro by pulling from a random list of encouragement text and have Tasker's Say action speak phrases like "Way to go!" and "Nice job." Take this concept further by pulling down famous quotes or a fortune cookie text generator from a free web service API like the one found on http://iheartquotes.com/api, convert the text to speech, and be surprised by what your Android device will say to you.

In the next chapter, we will combine the Tasker knowledge we've acquired with the scripting power of Python to create several neat programs that send and receive messages such as emails, instant messages, and even Twitter postings in a distraction-free way.

CHAPTER 8

Messaging Projects

We previously learned about how to create tasks with Tasker, scripts with SL4A, and native applications with AIDE. In this chapter, we are going to combine tasks and scripts so that we may benefit from the strengths of each. That is because Tasker has the ability to pass values to and from SL4A scripts. Both can be used for prototyping and refining apps that we choose to convert to native programs with a tool like AIDE or keep in perpetual, iterative development with the tasks and scripts being run.

Let's begin with a project that leverages the power of an SL4A-hosted Python script with the easy-to-use task management of Tasker. If you're like me, this simple project will also be one of the most used scripts throughout the day.

8.1 Check Email

This project will run a Python script to check for new email messages and speak their subject lines should any messages arrive in the inbox. We will use Tasker to schedule the script to run at regular intervals as well as make it easy to run from the home screen via a Tasker widget.

Because I prefer to listen to music or podcasts while commuting, working out, or cleaning the house, I'm often wearing headphones. Any chance I can hear information without having to dig out my phone to do so is a great time-saver. Email is one of the primary reasons I carry around a smartphone, even more so than voice calls or SMS messages. Yet I find it maddening to hear an email notification chime sound during my commute, dig the phone out of my case, unlock the screen, and bring up the email client only to discover that a spam message arrived.

While this project won't reduce spam, it will reduce the number of steps necessary to discover whether you have received such a message. It will also do an awesome job of helping you decide whether a message is important enough to stop what you're doing and immediately respond.

Scripting with Python

As we saw in Chapter 5, *Scripting with SL4A*, on page 63, SL4A can host a variety of scripting languages. I chose the Python scripting language with the projects in this book for a few reasons. First, Python is an easy language to understand thanks to its simple, well-formatted syntax and intuitive style. Second, its distribution is often referred to as one with "batteries included" because it bundles several powerful features in its standard library that other languages require as separate installations.

For example, Python bundles libraries for SQLite (a portable SQL-capable database), built-in libraries for web protocols, email and instant messaging, and much more. Lastly, Python is my personal favorite scripting language. Even though languages like Ruby are beautiful, there is just something about the engineering practicality of Python that appeals to my nuts-and-bolts tinkering mentality.

We will begin by writing and testing the Python script for checking and reading email. Once the script is working, we will tie it into the Talking Clock Tasker profile we created previously. We will also create a Task widget for easy access to the script. This widget will allow us to execute the script with a single touch vs. having to open SL4A, scroll through a list of scripts, select the checkmail.py file, and then the run script sprocket icon.

Check Mail Setup

Before we can write a script to check email, we need a mail server that supports the open protocols that Python's mail libraries encapsulate. While a variety of protocols can be used to access email, this script will be written with secure Internet Message Access Protocol (IMAP) in mind. This is the same protocol that Google and other free Internet email services offer. So, if you don't already have a secure IMAP-capable email account, you will need to create one for this script to work.

If you're able to access the Google Play market on your Android device, you already have a Gmail account. You can use that account or create a new account specifically for the purposes of testing and tweaking this script. Secure IMAP is not normally enabled by default in Gmail. To do so, log into your Gmail account via a web browser and select the Settings menu option after clicking the sprocket icon. From there, choose the Forwarding and POP/IMAP menu. Then select the Enable IMAP button. You can leave the other options at their default values. Upon doing so, your screen should look similar to Figure 66, *Gmail IMAP-enabled settings*, on page 117.

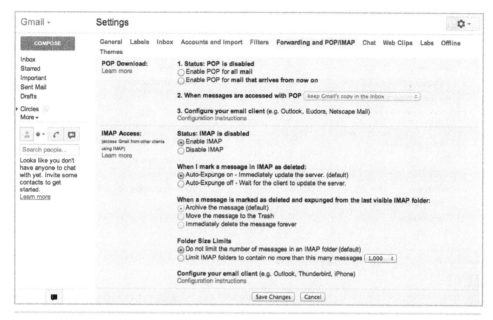

Figure 66—Gmail IMAP-enabled settings

The script we write will work with any secure IMAP standards-based service, not just Gmail. But for the purposes of our demonstration, Gmail should be more than adequate. Regardless of which service you use, make sure you can access it via an IMAP-capable email client first. The standard Mail client on Android is IMAP-capable, and you can use it to verify that secure IMAP on your email server of choice is properly configured.

To do so, open the Mail application on your Android device and choose the Settings menu option. Then select the Add Account label. In the setup screen, enter your username and password for the IMAP server of choice, and select the Manual Setup button, followed by the IMAP button on the next screen. The settings for Gmail secure IMAP are shown in Figure 67, *Gmail secure IMAP client settings*, on page 118. While not required for our purposes, you can also configure the Simple Mail Transport Protocol (SMTP) settings on the next screen. For example, Gmail uses secure SMTP over port 465 (Gmail can also use port 587), as shown in Figure 68, *Gmail secure SMTP client settings*, on page 118.

Accept the settings, and accept the defaults for the next screen as well. Give the account a name, such as IMAP Email Test. If you already had messages in your Gmail inbox, they should show up in the Inbox on your Android device.

Figure 67—Gmail secure IMAP client settings

Figure 68—Gmail secure SMTP client settings

You can also send yourself a message to that Gmail address to see whether it is received and displayed properly.

Once you have confirmed that the IMAP server and login settings are working, we can create the Python script that will check for unread messages in the Inbox. If any are located, the script will have our Android device speak the subjects of each unread message identified.

Check Mail Script

Assuming you have installed SL4A and the Python interpreter as discussed in Chapter 5, *Scripting with SL4A*, on page 63, launch SL4A. Create a new Python script by selecting the Add icon from the main SL4A menu and select Python 2.6.2 (or whatever version of the Python interpreter you installed on your device). Name the new Python script checkmail.py. SL4A has already imported the android library and created a new android object called droid.

Let's begin by importing several Python libraries (that we will call upon) into this file. These include the email, imaplib, re (regular expressions), and sys (system) libraries. Fortunately, these are all included in Python's standard library, so there is no need to download and install additional Python modules to bring these capabilities into our script.

Messaging/checkmail.py
```
import imaplib, email, re, sys
import android

droid = android.Android()
```

Next, let's try connecting to the IMAP server (in our example, we'll use Gmail) and navigate to our email Inbox. Notice the use of the word *try* in the last sentence. We will use Python's try-except block to wrap around the server connection logic. If we fail to connect to the server, we can catch the exception and have Android tell us that there was a problem connecting to the server.

Messaging/checkmail.py
```
try:
  server = imaplib.IMAP4_SSL('imap.gmail.com')
  server.login('MY_GMAIL_USER_NAME', 'MY_GMAIL_PASSWORD')
  mailboxes = server.list()
  server.select("INBOX")
except:
  droid.ttsSpeak("There was a problem connecting to the server.")
  sys.exit()
```

Assuming that the connection to the server was successful and we were able to locate and focus on the Inbox, we can scan the Inbox for unread messages. The code we use will incorporate the power of regular expressions to efficiently identify and parse any unread messages in our Inbox. If you are unfamiliar with using regular expressions, *Mastering Regular Expressions [Fri97]* by Jeffrey E. F. Friedl is a good resource to start reading about their practical use. Let's take a look at the code used to retrieve and read email messages.

Messaging/checkmail.py
```
   try:
❶   unread_messages = server.search(None, "UNSEEN")[1][0].split()
❷   unread_count = len(unread_messages)
❸   if unread_count == 1:
       droid.ttsSpeak(str(unread_count) + " unread message.")
     elif unread_count == 0:
       droid.ttsSpeak("No unread messages.")
     else:
       droid.ttsSpeak(str(unread_count) + "unread messages.")

❹     for item in unread_messages:
       droid.ttsSpeak("Message " + str(item) + ".")
       typ, message_content = server.fetch(str(item), '(RFC822)')
❺       for response in message_content:
```

```
    if isinstance(response, tuple):
        message = email.message_from_string(response[1])
        for header in ['FROM', 'SUBJECT']:
            droid.ttsSpeak(str(header.upper()) + " " + \
            str(re.sub(r'<.*>', "", message[header])))
```

❼ **except**:
```
    droid.ttsSpeak("There was a problem parsing the messages.")
```

❶ Using the IMAP UNSEEN command, we search the server for new messages by using the Python IMAP library's search function. Then we use split() on the results to separate each message independently.

❷ Here we capture the length of the unread_messages array so Android can tell us how many unread messages there are in our Inbox.

❸ Since there can be zero, one, or more unread messages that have been identified in our Inbox, we have Android tell us via SL4A's ttsSpeak() function in a grammatically correct way.

❹ The For loop iterates through our unread_messages array so that we can parse who the message was from and what is contained within the subject of the message. While we could also parse out the body of the message, I have found that this is burdensome (especially when the email is spam). If I know both the sender and the subject, I can often tell based on the sender and subject if a message requires my immediate attention.

❺ After speaking the message number and retrieving the message from the mail server via the Python IMAP fetch() function, we deconstruct the parts of the message in order to parse it for the message subject and sender.

❻ Since we're interested only in the email subject and sender, we need to parse the email message header only. Note the use of the regular expression function re.sub(r'<.*>', "", message[header])). This searches for and replaces the email address with a blank string. We do this so we don't have to listen to Android say both the sender's name and email address. If you have ever looked at the raw source of an email message, you will see that the person sending the message is listed as Sender Name <sender_email_address@theirdomain.com>. Since we often know people primarily by their names, not their email addresses, it's unnecessary and redundant to have Android speak both their names and their email addresses to us.

❼ If we have a problem retrieving or parsing the messages, we can gracefully exit the routine by having Android inform us that there was a problem doing so.

Save the checkmail.py file by selecting Android's back button. SL4A will display a dialog asking whether you would like to save the file, as shown in the figure here. Select Yes to do so.

Before we run the script, send the target email address with two or three test messages. That way, we can verify that the script not only connects to the mail server but also properly identifies and reads the subject lines of our test messages. Also, it should go without saying that you should check to make sure you have an active Internet connection before testing the script.

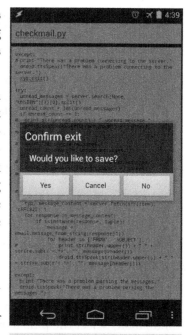

Figure 69—Save the checkmail.py script.

Now select the checkmail.py script from the list. This will pop up a row of icons, as shown in Figure 70, *Executing the checkmail.py script*. Select the sprocket icon to run the script. If everything goes according to plan, your Android device should tell you how many unread messages you have in your Inbox and proceed to read the subject lines of each unread message that it encountered. If there was a problem with either connecting to the server or parsing the messages, your Android will let you know that too.

With the checkmail.py script working, we can use Tasker to run the script periodically to check on the status of unread email messages. Since we already built a task that runs every fifteen minutes, we don't need to create a separate Tasker profile to execute this task at set time intervals. We already have a profile that we created for the Talking Clock task, so let's take advantage of this by adding onto an existing Tasker task.

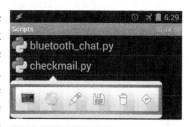

Figure 70—Executing the checkmail.py script

Tasker Integration

Let's create a new stand-alone task for the Check Mail script. This way, we'll have the flexibility to reuse the Check Mail routine in other tasks. We'll also be able to assign the Check Mail task to a widget, allowing us to check for

Wait...Just a Little Bit Longer

If you have a lot of unread email messages in your Inbox, your script will take a long time to complete its execution. Consequently, Android might complain with a dialog box asking if you want to wait or kill the task that is taking so long to complete. This is because Android doesn't like processes tying up system resources, especially those that might make the user interface unresponsive.

However, as we'll see when we wire up this script to other tasks, we won't have the luxury of waiting around until the script finishes. That's not a bad thing, since we probably don't want to listen to more than a minute or so of email senders and subjects. Also, it's not nice to tie up Android with background processes that don't quickly finish up their tasks.

unread messages whenever we want rather than waiting for the fifteen-minute interval to run.

Create a new task and call it Check Email. This task will consist of a single action, running the checkmail.py Python script. To add this action to the Check Email task, select the plus icon in the middle of Tasker's lower toolbar. Select the Script action, and then choose Run SL4A Script. Touch the Edit button and then choose the checkmail.py file. This will be the script that the SL4A action will execute when the Check Email task runs.

We could stop here, but I prefer to add a conditional statement to this task. If I know my Android phone is not connected to a network, then there is no reason to attempt to run the script. Doing so will produce the same result, with Android speaking, "There was a problem connecting to the server." To be even more specific, I chose to have the script run only when WiFi is turned on.

We can also opt to check whether we have 3G connectivity using the same technique, but let's keep it simple for now and just check to see whether the WiFi radio is on. To do so, check the If box in the SL4A Action Edit task and test to see whether the %WIFI variable matches the On state. And even though it's not necessary in this single step task, I usually enable the Continue Task After Error checkbox to keep the rest of the task running in case the SL4A script execution fails. Your configured SL4A task should look like the one shown in Figure 71, *The checkmail.py SL4A action in Tasker*, on page 123.

Save your changes by selecting the Action Edit label in the upper-left corner of the screen. Then confirm that the task has been configured correctly by selecting the Run icon on the left side of the lower toolbar in the Check Email Task Edit screen. If it didn't run, make sure your WiFi radio is turned on.

One more thing I like to do with my tasks is assign them a relevant icon. Not only does this assist as a visual reminder of what the task does, but Tasker also uses that assigned icon when creating a widget from the chosen task. In this case, touch the image select icon in the lower-right side of the bottom task toolbar.

You can use an existing application icon (the Android Email application icon for example), but that's not a good idea since it might get confusing on the home screen if both the Email application and the Check Mail widget have the same icon. Instead, I used an envelope icon in Android-friendly .png format that I found on Iconfinder.com.

With the working individual Check Email task defined, we can add it to the Talking Clock task we created earlier. To do so, open the Talking Clock task in Tasker and add a new action to it by selecting the plus icon.

Then, just as we did previously with the Battery Status task, choose the Task action category followed by the Perform Task action. Then select the magnifying glass icon to choose the Check Email task from the pop-up dialog box that lists all the tasks you have created so far in Tasker. When done, the Check Email Perform Task dialog should look similar to the one shown in Figure 72, *The Check Email Perform Task action in Tasker*.

Select the Task Edit label in the upper-left corner of the screen to save your changes. Now run the Talking Clock script. Assuming the WiFi radio is on, you should hear your Android device speak the time, followed shortly thereafter with a tally of unread messages and the sender and subject of those unread emails. However, you will quickly notice that if the email reading goes on longer than a minute or so, Tasker ends the checkmail.py Python script, often in mid-sentence. Alas, this is one of the limitations we can't easily address.

Figure 71—The checkmail.py SL4A action in Tasker

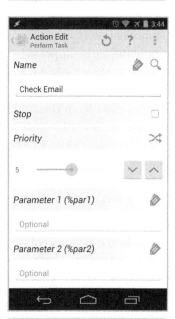

Figure 72—The Check Email Perform Task action in Tasker

But as I mentioned earlier, I don't mind that Tasker puts the brakes on the running script. If I have a stack of unread emails waiting for me, I am going to have to respond to some of them anyway. So, while the task doesn't perform exactly as intended, I honestly like the fact that Tasker takes command and stops the script on my behalf. If this isn't the kind of behavior you appreciate, you can always consider going native and converting the Check Email task to a native Android application like we did in Chapter 6, *Programming with AIDE*, on page 75.

Another more annoying limitation of the Check Email script, as well as any SL4A script in general, is that it stops video playback when it executes. If you happen to be watching a YouTube or other media player video when the script launches, video playback will halt and require you to manually unpause the playback to continue. It's literally a showstopper. Ideally this problem can be fixed in a future SL4A update.

Before we move on to our next project, let's make the Check Email function accessible via a Tasker widget so we can easily run it from the Android home screen.

Check Mail Widget

Similar to the steps we used in Section 7.2, *Pomodoro Widget Redux*, on page 98, we will apply the same approach to exposing the Check Email Tasker task as a widget. Doing so is a simple two-step process. First, select the Tasker Task widget from the Android Widgets selection screen, as we did with the Pomodoro widget, and then select the Check Email task from the list of tasks you have on your phone. For example, my list of Tasker tasks looks like the one shown in the figure here.

Tasker will then present you with the steps of the selected task as confirmation that this is the task you want to assign to the widget. Select the Task Widget/Check Email label in the upper left corner of the screen to confirm the assignment. The envelope icon we previously assigned to the Check Email task will appear on the home

Figure 73—A selection of Tasker tasks

screen. Now you can easily run the Check Email task at any time by touching the Check Email widget envelope icon.

Another even cooler approach you can take with the Check Email task is to assign it to a Headset Button Controller action. In my case, I have set a four-button press on my middle headset hardware button to trigger the action to run the Check Email script.

To do so, launch the Headset Button Controller program and select Quadruple Click from the Easy tab. Select "Tasker task" from the pop-up list, as shown in the figure here.

For longer clicks like these, I recommend leaving the "Play beep sound" checkbox enabled as an audio cue that you have indeed tapped the headset hardware button four times. Then, just as we did with the task widget assignment, select the Check Email task from the Tasker task list. Once the assignment is configured, test it by plugging in your headset and tapping the headset hardware button four times. Doing so should launch the Check Email Tasker task that will in turn run the checkemail.py Python SL4A script. Now whenever you're on the go and want to check for new email without having to reach for your smartphone, just tap your headset button four times to hear any new email messages you may have received. Now that's pretty cool!

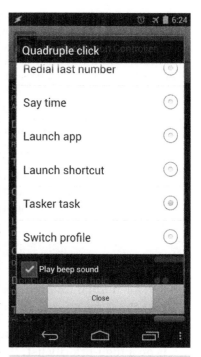

Figure 74—Assigning a Tasker task to a quadruple-click

Enhancements

The aforementioned SL4A limitations notwithstanding, think about the kind of improvements that could be made to the Check Email project. Here are some ways to add upon the foundation we built:

- Minimize the reading of spam by filtering out message readings from unknown sources. Create an array of approved senders and iterate through it to verify that the sender is in the list before retrieving and reading the subject.

Tasker Task Widget vs. SL4A Script Shortcut

If you have been exploring SL4A a bit on your own, you may have come across the ability to create shortcuts to either edit or run your SL4A scripts. If so, you may be wondering why I am going through the trouble of creating Tasker task widgets when the SL4A script shortcuts do nearly the same thing. That is, both will launch the target script when the assigned icon is touched on the home screen.

There are two reasons why I prefer using the Tasker Task widget above the SL4A script shortcut. First, Tasker allows you to assign an icon to the task that the widget will run. SL4A uses the same language-specific icon for the shortcut, making it hard to quickly identify by sight which shortcut launches which script. And while most Android third-party launchers such as Nova Launcher allow you to swap out a home-screen icon with an alternate of your choice, you lose these icon assignments if you switch to a different launcher or revert to the stock Android home-screen settings.

The second and more important advantage of using Tasker to encapsulate each SL4A script into a distinct task is so that they can be easily mixed and matched with other Tasker tasks. For example, if you have already built an SL4A script that parses HTML tags, you can easily reuse that in a future Tasker task that may require that functionality. As you amass a library of Tasker tasks and SL4A scripts, you will appreciate how much easier it is to manage and organize these functional assets under a single umbrella.

- Prioritize message reading based on the sender. Have two lists of names, one for normal and one for high priority, and rearrange the subjects so that those received from high-priority senders are read first.

- Add the option to read the message body, especially if the message sender is on a high-priority list. If the subject is important or intriguing, Android can ask "Would you like me to read the full message?" We will learn how to interactively respond to scripted conditions using just our voice in the next project.

- Add the ability to respond to a message via speech-to-text conversion. We will learn how to do this in the next project.

8.2 Speak 'n' Tweet

Keeping with the theme of hands-free audio-delivered data exchange, our next project will post a speech-to-text translation to your Twitter timeline. Select a widget or a few clicks of your headset hardware button, wait for the audio cue to speak, say what you want posted, and Android will convert your speech to text, confirm what you said, post it to your Twitter account, and read back to you what was just posted. Just as we did with the Check Email project, we're going to employ both SL4A and Tasker, with Tasker serving as a container to let us call the SL4A Python script from a widget or headset button press.

If you took the time to explore the contents of the Python libraries included in the Python for Android distribution, you may have discovered that it includes a Twitter library. Unfortunately, that library is outdated because it uses an old username/password authentication scheme that Twitter has since replaced with the OAuth authentication standard scheme. OAuth is far more secure than the old username/password approach, but it is also far more complex to configure. In fact, we will spend far more time creating and configuring the OAuth credentials for this project than writing the speech-translation and tweet-posting Python script.

The Tweepy Library

Since the Twitter library included in the Python for Android distribution won't work with OAuth, we need to replace it with a Python Twitter library that is OAuth-aware. We can do this by adding a pure Python Twitter library to the Python distribution that was installed on our Android device. However, the important point to keep in mind about this approach is that it works only when using pure Python libraries that don't require platform-specific compilation to call upon external system-level OS features.

Visit the Tweepy library page on GitHub and click the Download ZIP button. Proceed to download and extract the Tweepy library from the project's GitHub repository. Since Tweepy (and many other third-party Python libraries) are designed to be distributed via popular Python package deployment tools such as easy_install or pip, there are a lot of extra setup files that don't need to be copied to the extras Python directory on our Android device. All we really need is the extracted tweepy directory. Copy that directory to your Android device. The easiest way to do this is to use Google's Android File Transfer tool that was mentioned in *Choosing an Audio Clip*, on page 99.

Connect your Android device to your computer and, if it didn't automatically start, launch the Android File Transfer utility. Expand the com.googlecode.python-forandroid directory, followed by the extras directory and then the python directory. This is where our Python for Android libraries reside. Copy the tweepy folder to this location. Note that Figure 75, *Location of Python library files*, on page 128 doesn't show the entire contents of the python directory, and it also shows the tweepy directory already copied into the proper location.

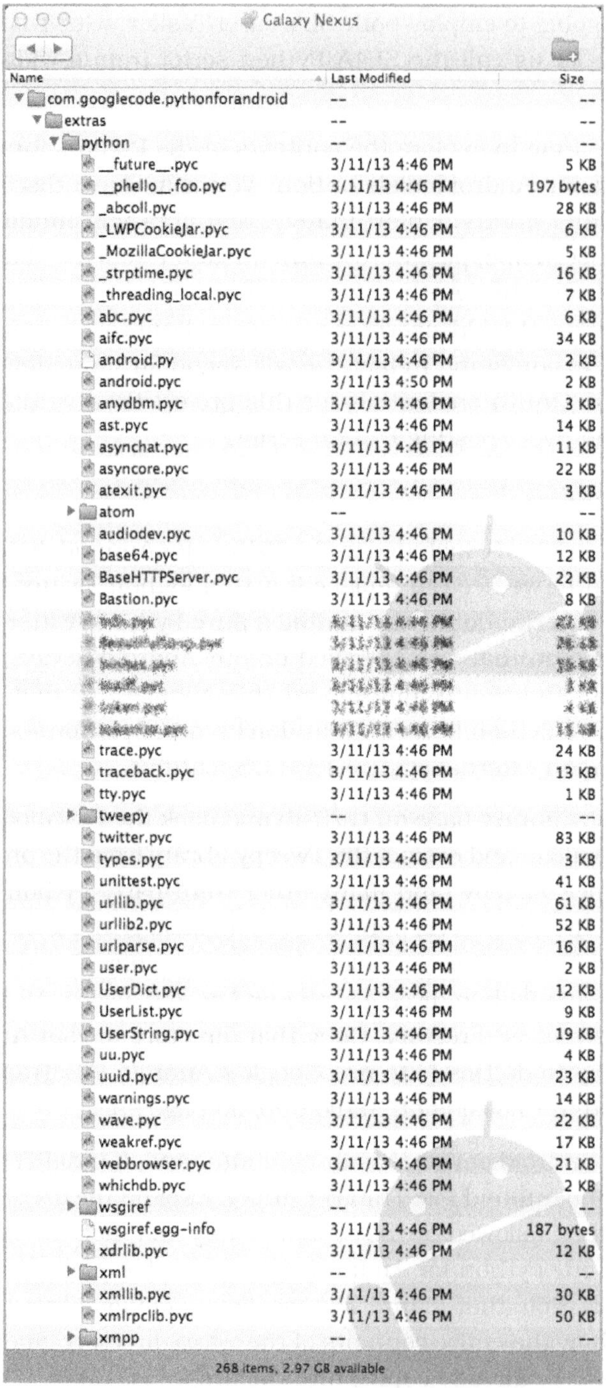

Name	Last Modified	Size
▼ com.googlecode.pythonforandroid	--	--
▼ extras	--	--
▼ python	--	--
__future__.pyc	3/11/13 4:46 PM	5 KB
__phello__.foo.pyc	3/11/13 4:46 PM	197 bytes
_abcoll.pyc	3/11/13 4:46 PM	28 KB
_LWPCookieJar.pyc	3/11/13 4:46 PM	6 KB
_MozillaCookieJar.pyc	3/11/13 4:46 PM	5 KB
_strptime.pyc	3/11/13 4:46 PM	16 KB
_threading_local.pyc	3/11/13 4:46 PM	7 KB
abc.pyc	3/11/13 4:46 PM	6 KB
aifc.pyc	3/11/13 4:46 PM	34 KB
android.py	3/11/13 4:46 PM	2 KB
android.pyc	3/11/13 4:50 PM	2 KB
anydbm.pyc	3/11/13 4:46 PM	3 KB
ast.pyc	3/11/13 4:46 PM	14 KB
asynchat.pyc	3/11/13 4:46 PM	11 KB
asyncore.pyc	3/11/13 4:46 PM	22 KB
atexit.pyc	3/11/13 4:46 PM	3 KB
▶ atom	--	--
audiodev.pyc	3/11/13 4:46 PM	10 KB
base64.pyc	3/11/13 4:46 PM	12 KB
BaseHTTPServer.pyc	3/11/13 4:46 PM	22 KB
Bastion.pyc	3/11/13 4:46 PM	8 KB
trace.pyc	3/11/13 4:46 PM	24 KB
traceback.pyc	3/11/13 4:46 PM	13 KB
tty.pyc	3/11/13 4:46 PM	1 KB
▶ tweepy	--	--
twitter.pyc	3/11/13 4:46 PM	83 KB
types.pyc	3/11/13 4:46 PM	3 KB
unittest.pyc	3/11/13 4:46 PM	41 KB
urllib.pyc	3/11/13 4:46 PM	61 KB
urllib2.pyc	3/11/13 4:46 PM	52 KB
urlparse.pyc	3/11/13 4:46 PM	16 KB
user.pyc	3/11/13 4:46 PM	2 KB
UserDict.pyc	3/11/13 4:46 PM	12 KB
UserList.pyc	3/11/13 4:46 PM	9 KB
UserString.pyc	3/11/13 4:46 PM	19 KB
uu.pyc	3/11/13 4:46 PM	4 KB
uuid.pyc	3/11/13 4:46 PM	23 KB
warnings.pyc	3/11/13 4:46 PM	14 KB
wave.pyc	3/11/13 4:46 PM	22 KB
weakref.pyc	3/11/13 4:46 PM	17 KB
webbrowser.pyc	3/11/13 4:46 PM	21 KB
whichdb.pyc	3/11/13 4:46 PM	2 KB
▶ wsgiref	--	--
wsgiref.egg-info	3/11/13 4:46 PM	187 bytes
xdrlib.pyc	3/11/13 4:46 PM	12 KB
▶ xml	--	--
xmllib.pyc	3/11/13 4:46 PM	30 KB
xmlrpclib.pyc	3/11/13 4:46 PM	50 KB
▶ xmpp	--	--

268 items, 2.97 GB available

Figure 75—Location of Python library files

SL4A Python Libraries

If you were to try to install a nifty Python workflow library called Fabric,[a] it wouldn't work by just copying the Fabric Python files into your project. That's because Fabric relies on a cryptographic library called PyCrypto that requires a natively compiled library to execute its cryptographic functions.[b] In this case, the SL4A community has recognized the importance of this library and made the effort to natively compile the PyCrypto library as a separate download.[c]

For the adventurous and determined Python and Android programmer, there exists a way to create these natively compiled Python libraries packages for use on Android that involves the Android Native Development Kit (NDK) and a fair amount of native Android and C++ development expertise. That said, it's easier to search for a pure Python library than to attempt to compile one that relies on native system code. In the case of our need for a pure Python OAuth-capable Twitter library, such a solution exists in a project called Tweepy.[d]

a.   http://fabfile.org
b.   https://www.dlitz.net/software/pycrypto/
c.   http://code.google.com/p/python-for-android/wiki/Modules
d.   https://github.com/tweepy/tweepy

With these files in place, you're ready to import the Tweepy library into your own projects. But before we actually use the Tweepy library, we need a Twitter developer account and the appropriate OAuth keys, tokens, and secret values to authenticate an OAuth session with the Twitter service.

OAuth Credentials

To obtain the four keys to the Twitter application kingdom (the consumer key, consumer secret, access token, and access secret), visit the Twitter Developers apps website.[1] You can sign in with your existing Twitter account or create a new account specifically for your Twitter applications. Since this project is intended for your own personal use rather than an application that will be distributed in the Play store, feel free to log in with your own Twitter account login credentials.

Select the "Create a new application" button. Fill out the form with the required fields (unique name, app description at least ten characters long, and your website URL), agree to the terms of use, supply the CAPTCHA values, and select the "Create your Twitter application" button.

---

1.   https://dev.twitter.com/apps

Assuming you entered the information correctly, you should see a page listing the details of the Twitter application you just created, including the OAuth settings. By default, new applications are created with a read-only access level, as shown in the next figure.

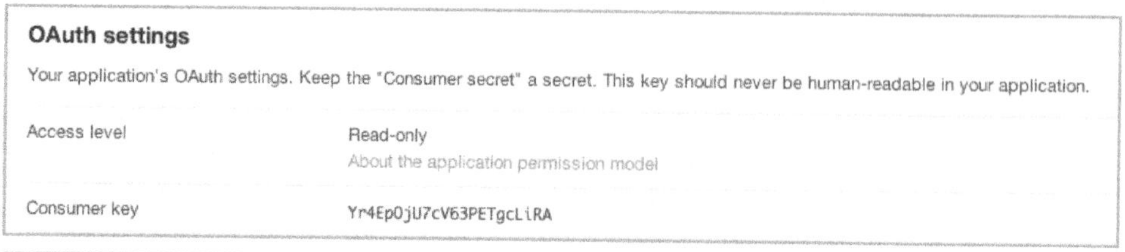

OAuth settings

Your application's OAuth settings. Keep the "Consumer secret" a secret. This key should never be human-readable in your application.

Access level	Read-only
	About the application permission model
Consumer key	Yr4EpOjU7cV63PETgcLiRA

Figure 76—Apps set to read-only by default

We need to change this permission to read-write since our Python script will be posting tweets to our timeline. To do so, select the Settings tab at the top of the web page and scroll down to the application type. Change the value from read-only to read-write, as shown in Figure 77, *Setting the app type to read-write*. Then select the "Update this Twitter application's settings" button on the bottom of the page to update the access level.

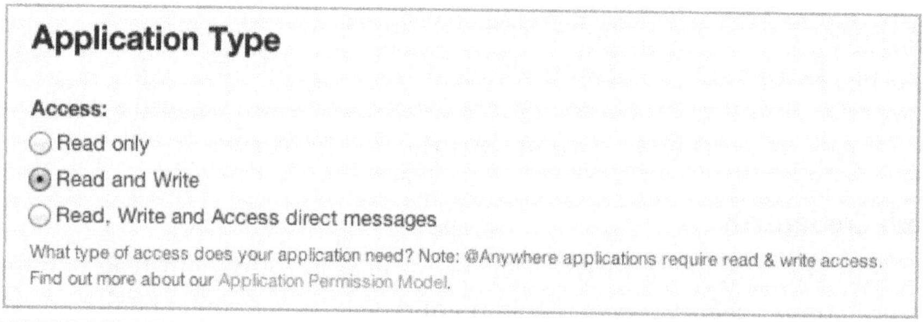

Application Type

Access:
○ Read only
● Read and Write
○ Read, Write and Access direct messages

What type of access does your application need? Note: @Anywhere applications require read & write access. Find out more about our Application Permission Model.

Figure 77—Setting the app type to read-write

Return to the application details screen by selecting the Details tab at the top of the page. Confirm that the application access level has been set to read-write, as shown in Figure 78, *OAuth access set to read-write*, on page 131.

We have one more step to do before we can authenticate a Tweepy session. We need to generate an access token and its secret. Twitter has made this easy for dedicated apps like ours. Simply select the "Create my access token" button on the Details page, and Twitter will automatically generate these for the Twitter account you used to log into the developer website. These credentials cannot be used with other Twitter logins, so if you want to use the application's consumer key and secret with a different Twitter account, you

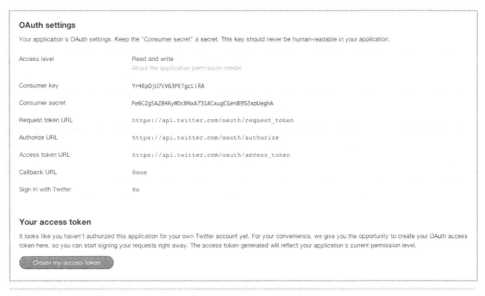

Figure 78—OAuth access set to read-write

will have to generate an access token and secret specific to that account. For our script, we will use the access token and secret that Twitter generated for us. Take a look at this example, keeping in mind that your token values will be different from the ones shown in the screenshots.

Figure 79—OAuth access tokens

Now that we have all four values required for OAuth authentication, we can move on to writing our Tweepy-powered SL4A Python script.

Speak Tweet Script

The SL4A Python script we will create for this project will import the Tweepy library to authenticate and post our spoken tweets to our Twitter timeline.

We will also leverage Python for Android's Android library to capture and convert our speech to text for both tweet entry and posting confirmation.

Open SL4A, add a new Python script, name it speaktweet.py, and begin by importing the required modules. In addition to the default Android module that SL4A already included for us, we will import the sys, tweepy, and time libraries. The reason for including the time library is because we will need the script to wait for Android to stop talking before we can ask it to capture our voice for translation.

Messaging/speaktweet.py
```
import time, tweepy, sys
import android
droid = android.Android()
```

Next, we're going to make a call to the Android recognizeSpeech() function to capture and convert our speech. Then we will have Android say back to us what it converted using the ttsSpeak() function. Android will then ask us whether this is the tweet we want to post. This is important because although the speech-to-text capabilities of Android are amazing, they're not perfect. This step allows us to confirm the accuracy of the tweet before it gets posted. However, we have to wait until Android is done speaking the tweet in question before it can listen for a response, which is why we need to ask the script to wait using the time.sleep(1) function. If we agree to the phrase captured, we can allow the script to continue its execution. Any other response will exit the program.

Messaging/speaktweet.py
```
while True:
    tweet = str(droid.recognizeSpeech().result)
    droid.ttsSpeak("I heard " + tweet + ". Is this what you want to post?")
    while droid.ttsIsSpeaking()[1] is True:
        time.sleep(1)

    response = str(droid.recognizeSpeech().result)
    if response == "yes":
        break
    else:
        droid.ttsSpeak("The post has been cancelled.")
        sys.exit()
```

If we respond with a spoken "Yes" that Android recognized, the next step is to authenticate to our Twitter account using our OAuth credentials. Set the consumer key, consumer secret, access token, and access token secret values and pass these to Tweepy's OAuthHander function.

Messaging/speaktweet.py

```
consumer_key = "YOUR_CONSUMER_KEY_GOES_HERE"
consumer_secret = "YOUR_CONSUMER_KEY_SECRET_GOES_HERE"

access_token = "YOUR_ACCESS_TOKEN_GOES_HERE"
access_token_secret = "YOUR_ACCESS_TOKEN_SECRET_GOES_HERE"

auth = tweepy.OAuthHandler(consumer_key, consumer_secret)
auth.set_access_token(access_token, access_token_secret)
```

Google's speech-to-text service does a nice job in this case, but it doesn't make implicit assumptions about punctuation and sentence structure. If you were to post the converted text as is, your post would be in lowercase and be missing a period at the end of the sentence. We'll fix that before the text gets posted by making the first letter in the tweet string uppercase and adding a period to the end of the string.

Messaging/speaktweet.py

```
tweet = tweet[0].upper() + tweet[1:] + '.'
```

With the sentence properly formatted, we can finally authenticate to Twitter and post the tweet. If the tweet was successfully posted, Android will tell us so. If the tweet didn't get posted, whether because of a network problem or authentication error, Android will let us know that too.

Messaging/speaktweet.py

```
try:
    api = tweepy.API(auth)
    api.update_status(tweet)
    droid.ttsSpeak(tweet[:-1] + " has been posted to your Twitter timeline.")
except:
    droid.ttsSpeak("There was a problem connecting to the server.")
    sys.exit()
```

Save the speaktweet.py file, make sure your Android device has a connection to the Internet, and give the script a try. Select the file from the SL4A Scripts screen; then select the sprocket icon to run the script. A chime will sound indicating that Android is recording your voice. Speak a brief test phrase like "Hello, world." Android should respond with "I heard 'Hello, world.' Is this what you want to post?" If that's not the phrase that was spoken back to you, a "No" response will cancel the post and exit the script. If Android did speak the phrase correctly, responding with a "Yes" will allow the script to proceed.

Assuming you entered your OAuth values correctly into the script and the Twitter service is network accessible, the next phrase you should hear spoken from your Android device is "Hello, world has been posted to your Twitter timeline." Confirm this statement by visiting your Twitter page and reviewing your most recent posts. There you should see a recently added "Hello world." entry on your Twitter timeline. Awesome!

Now let's make the speaktweet.py script more easily accessible to Tasker tasks and on the Android home screen by wrapping it in a Tasker task and widget, just like we previously did for the Check Email project.

Tasker Wrapper

Following the same procedure we used for the Check.Email Tasker integration, open Tasker and create a new task called Speak Tweet. The task will host a single action, running the speaktweet.py SL4A Python script. Add the action by selecting the plus icon in the lower Task Edit toolbar. Select the Script Action Category followed by the Run SL4A Script action. Touch the magnifying glass icon in the Action Edit Name field and choose the speaktweet.py file from the list. Save the action by selecting the Action Edit label in the upper left of the screen.

While we're in the Task Edit screen, let's also assign an icon for the task so we'll be able to easily identify it when we create the Tasker widget for the script. I chose a free Twitter .png-formatted icon from the IconFinder website. To set the icon, select the checkerboard icon in the lower-right corner of the Task Edit toolbar. In my case, the Twitter icon I used was a Local Media file. Navigate to the file path of the icon and set it by selecting the icon file of choice.

With the icon configured, we can save the Speak Tweet task by selecting the Task Edit label in the upper-left corner of the Task Edit screen. Verify that the script has been correctly configured by running the Speak Tweet task. Your results should be the same as before when you ran the script within the SL4A shell.

Now that the Tasker Task has been created, we can either call upon it within a Tasker widget or assign it to a headset button action using the Headset Button Controller program. To set up a widget, add a new widget on your home screen and select the Tasker Task widget from the list. From there, choose the Speak Tweet task from the Task Selection pop-up list. Verify that the task you chose is correct and select the Task label in the upper-left corner of the screen to set the Speak Tweet task widget on your home page. If you used the free Twitter icon from the IconFinder website, your Speak Tweet widget may look similar to mine, as shown in Figure 80, *The Speak Tweet widget*, on page 135. Now you'll be able to run the Speak Tweet task directly from your home screen by selecting the Speak Tweet widget!

Finally, let's assign the click of our headset button to the Speak Tweet task. Choose how many clicks you prefer. For the sake of this project, let's assign it to four clicks of the headset button. Open the Headset Button Controller program and select the "Quadruple click" from the Easy tab. Choose the Tasker task followed by the Speak Tweet task from the Task Selection list. Save the changes, plug in your headset, and click the headset hardware button four times in a row. You should hear the familiar Android speech

Figure 80—The Speak Tweet widget

recognition indicator chime in your ears. Say what you want to tweet, acknowledge, and verify that the tweet was posted on your Twitter timeline.

If you're a frequent tweeter, imagine the convenience and ease by which you can now post tweets to your timeline. Want to notify your followers of what you're thinking about while walking to work? Tap your headset button and speak your mind.

Enhancements

We just built something straight out of a science-fiction story with a couple of lines of code. To think that we can speak a phrase into our mobile device and have it broadcast to the planet is just too cool. Here are a few ideas to make it even better:

- Add the ability to replace or expand text phrases based on your own set of keywords. So when you speak the word "smiley," Speak Tweet will replace the word with a :-) character string. Think of it as TextExpander for voice input.[2]

- Use the StreamListener function of the Tweepy library to listen to tweets being posted in real time by the accounts you follow on Twitter. Refer to the streamwatcher.py example from the Tweepy project GitHub page.[3]

- Enhance the script using Tweepy's friends_timeline() function by asking Android to "Read new tweets."

- Add geolocation data to your tweets by enabling the GPS radio and capturing and posting your coordinates. We will learn how to record and transmit GPS data in our next project.

---

2. http://smilesoftware.com/TextExpander/index.html
3. https://github.com/tweepy/examples/blob/master/streamwatcher.py

8.3   Jabber Tracker

The projects we have worked on so far in this chapter have used SL4A for code logic and Tasker as the shell and script execution scheduler. But Tasker can also be used to pass values it has acquired to SL4A scripts via Tasker's Pass Variables field in its Run SL4A Script action. Using the familiar Tasker variable name syntax of %NAME_OF_VARIABLE, we can supply our Python scripts with values for additional processing. We're going to take advantage of this feature in this project.

One of the many libraries included in the Python for Android bundle is for the Extensible Messaging and Presence instant messaging protocol (XMPP).[4] Historically referred to as the Jabber protocol, XMPP is used in a number of instant messaging clients for desktop and mobile devices. Apple Messages (formerly known as iChat) and Google Hangouts (formerly known as Google Talk) both use XMPP as a messaging protocol. In this project, we are going to tap into this capability by creating our own Jabber client that will transmit our location to a designated recipient as an instant message.

The task will run every ten minutes and embed a link prepopulated with the device's latitude and longitude to Google Maps. This will allow the message's recipient to click the link and see on a map exactly where the device is located whenever the script is running. While we're at it, we'll also send the current battery level so the recipient knows how much charge the Android device has remaining. This is important because the GPS radio has a tendency to aggressively deplete the battery. If the script stops sending an update, the last message might show why if the battery level reported was less than 10 percent charge remaining.

We will start with writing the XMPP message transmission script, and that will use a Jabber-aware instant messaging server to relay the message. Using valid IM account credentials, we will associate the account used in the Jabber Tracker with a recipient account that will receive the messages. Then we will create the Tasker task that will supply the Python script with current latitude and longitude values captured by the Android's GPS radio. Finally, we will take our Android for a test ride to see how well the tracking messages account for its location.

XMPP Client Account

If you have a Gmail account, you already have an XMPP client by default. Google Hangouts is an instant messaging client that uses standard XMPP to authenticate and communicate. Of course, if you would rather use a different

---

4.   http://xmpp.org

XMPP server, the iChat (aka Messages in OS X 10.8) server included with Apple's OS X server works. If you prefer Linux, you can install and run the open source Jabber server, which works perfectly with the client we will create as well. To learn more about installing a Jabber server and creating user accounts, check out the excellent ejabberd open source project.[5]

Let's keep things simple for now. Since we already used a Gmail account for the Check Mail project, we are going to use the Google Hangouts login associated with the Gmail account you used for it. Assuming you have already created a Gmail account, launch the Google Hangouts program on your Android device and log in with the same credentials you use for Gmail. This will be the instant messaging client that receives the inbound messages.

Next, visit http://gmail.google.com and create another Gmail account to be exclusively used for sending instant messages to your primary Gmail account. After you create the second account, you need to allow your primary account to receive messages from this second account. To do so, add the Gmail.com address of the second account to your Google Hangouts chat list via the Add Contact menu item. Once the invitation has been sent, log into Gmail with the second account and accept the Google Hangouts invitation. And with that, your primary and secondary Gmail accounts are associated with each other. You should now be able to verify this association by sending a test instant message from your secondary Gmail account to your primary account.

Now that you have two instant messaging accounts configured, one to send the instant message and one to receive it, we can use the account credentials for sending the message in our XMPP script.

The XMPP Python Script

The Python script for this project will do three simple tasks. The first will be to capture the current latitude and longitude values reported and supplied by Tasker. The second step will be to authenticate to the XMPP server. The final step will be to send a formatted XMPP message containing the geographic coordinates to a designated recipient. Since the GPS radio tends to consume battery charge quickly, we will also include the current battery status and timestamp in the instant message.

Thanks to the bundled XMPP Python library, authenticating to the XMPP server and sending an XMPP message takes only a few lines of code. We will start by taking a look at the full script.

---

5. http://www.ejabberd.im

Messaging/jabbertracker.py

```
❶ import android
   import random
   import xmpp

❷ droid = android.Android()
   location = droid.getIntent().result[u'extras'][u'%LOC']
   battery = droid.getIntent().result[u'extras'][u'%BATT']
   date = droid.getIntent().result[u'extras'][u'%DATE']
   time = droid.getIntent().result[u'extras'][u'%TIME']

❸ username = 'secondary_address@gmail.com'
   password = 'secondary_address_password'
   recipient = 'primary_address@gmail.com'

❹ uid = xmpp.protocol.JID(username)
   client = xmpp.Client(uid.getDomain(), debug=[])
   client.connect(server=('talk.google.com',5223))

   auth = client.auth(uid.getNode(), password, 'JabberTracker')

   client.sendInitPresence()
❺
   message = xmpp.Message(recipient,
                          'I am here: http://maps.google.com/maps?q='
                          + location + ' at ' + time + ' on ' + date
                          + '. Battery level at ' + battery + '%.')
   message.setAttr('type', 'chat')
❻ message.setAttr('id', random.randrange(1,10000000))
❼ client.send(message)
   client.disconnect()
```

This short yet powerful script performs the following functions:

❶ In addition to importing the obligatory Android library, we will pull in the XMPP library. This will allow us to authenticate and send a message via the XMPP server. We also need to pull in Python's random library to make up for a helpful but limiting feature of Google Hangouts that we discuss shortly in more detail.

❷ Here we initialize an Android object and assign it the droid variable. We need this object to obtain the geolocation data, battery level, date, and time from Tasker. Then we will create four variables (location, battery, date, and time) and assign the %LOC, %BATT, %DATE, and %TIME values that will be passed from Tasker to this script.

❸ In this segment, we assign the username, password, and message recipient variables in one easy-to-edit section. Be sure to replace the placeholder values with your own Gmail login credentials and the name of the paired recipient Google Hangouts account you want to send your instant messages to.

❹ This portion of the script creates the XMPP user identifier from the username and instructs the XMPP results to be output in verbose debug mode. That way, if we encounter problems with getting the script to run, we can examine the SL4A console output to review any errors that were encountered. We also connect the client to the XMPP server (in this case, talk.google.com) and the server's port number (in the case of Google Hangouts, which uses XMPP secure login, the port number is 5223). Once we're connected to the server, we authenticate our XMPP client login credentials with the server and prepare to transmit our instant message.

❺ This is where we format our XMPP message by incorporating the location and battery values passed from Tasker to the script. The location data will be incorporated into a Google Maps URL. Assuming that the message recipient is using a modern XMPP-compatible client like Apple iChat/ Messages, Google Hangouts, Pidgin, or similar applications, this URL will display the location pin icon in the browser.

❻ When we imported the random Python library earlier to create a random number, we did so because Google has incorporated a feature that filters out repeating messages. This way, if someone is accidentally sending the same instant message twice, the recipient sees the message only once. However, since we want to see all messages regardless of whether the message contents are identical, we need to bypass this message-filtering feature by assigning a unique message ID to each instant message we transmit. We do this by generating a random integer between one and ten million, assuring that the likelihood of generating the same message ID in the same user session is very low.

❼ With our message formatted with the contents and message ID type and attributes, we can finally send the message to the recipient. After the message has been transmitted, we disconnect from the XMPP server.

Remember to update the script with the login credentials of your secondary Gmail account and the address of your primary (message recipient) address. Save the changes to a file called jabbertracker.py to the sl4a/scripts directory on your Android device. But don't try running the script just yet. If you do, it will fail because it isn't receiving the latitude, longitude, date, and battery values being passed to it by Tasker. Let's work on fixing that now.

Geolocation Tasker Task

With the Python script done, we can create a new Tasker task called Jabber Tracker. Do so by selecting the plus icon in the Tasker task toolbar. Create an action that acquires the current location coordinates. To d this this, add a new action and once again select the Misc action category followed by the Get Location action. Accept the default values and save the action.

Now that the Jabber Tracker task has captured the current latitude and longitude location, we can pass those values to our jabbertracker.py script. Add a new action and select the Script Action Category followed by the Run SL4A Script item. In the Name field of the Run SL4A Script Action Edit screen, add jabbertracker.py. In the Pass Variables field, we want to have Tasker pass the four variables that jabbertracker.py expects to receive. These are %BATT, %LOC, %TIME, and %DATE. Once these variable names have been entered, the screen should look like Figure 81, *The jabbertracker.py Script Tasker action.*

Figure 81—The **jabbertracker.py** Script Tasker action

Figure 82—The Complete Jabber Tracker Tasker task

Save this action. With the Jabber Tracker task complete, it should look like Figure 82, *The Complete Jabber Tracker Tasker task.*

Now create a Tasker profile that will execute the Jabber Tracker task every ten minutes. Select the Profiles tab in Tasker, followed by the plus icon to create a new profile. Name the profile Jabber Tracker. Then choose Time from the pop-up menu. Deselect the From and To checkboxes and instead select and activate the Repeat checkbox. Set the profile to execute every ten minutes and save the changes. Lastly, choose the Jabber Tracker task that appears in the pop-up menu. When done, the Jabber Tracker profile should look like the one shown in Figure 83, *The Jabber Tracker Tasker profile*.

With the profile created and associated with the Jabber Tracker task, we are ready to test our handiwork.

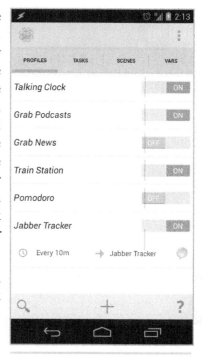

Figure 83—The Jabber Tracker Tasker profile

Testing the Tracker

You can choose to send and receive instant messages on the same device or use your Android to send messages and use a laptop or a different Android device to receive messages. I prefer to use the same device to keep debugging any problems simple.

To verify that you are in an area that can receive GPS signals, turn on your Android's GPS radio by toggling it on in the Location page within the Android Settings program. Then verify that your GPS radio is working correctly by launching Google Maps. Wait for the GPS signal to be acquired, and then ask Google Maps to determine your current location. Once confirmed, activate the Jabber Tracker profile and take your Android along for a walk, bike ride, or drive. You should see an instant message display on the recipient's IM application every ten minutes with the updated location, battery level, date, and time.

If ten minutes is too long or too short between transmissions, you can vary the frequency of executing the Jabber Tracker task by changing the Repeat Every value in the Jabber Tracker profile we created earlier. If you're using the Google Hangouts application on an Android device and are logged into it with the recipient's account, then your results may look similar to the ones shown in Figure 84, *Jabber Tracker instant messages*, on page 142.

Figure 84—Jabber Tracker instant messages

Figure 85—Android location as displayed in the Google Chrome Browser

When you select the URL, it will open whatever you have set as your default map display application on your Android device and show the location when the instant message was transmitted, as shown in Figure 85, *Android location as displayed in the Google Chrome Browser.*

Enhancements

The combination of geolocation and messaging is pretty powerful, but there are improvements we can add to make this project even more interesting. Here are just a few ideas to get started with:

- Take a photo with the camera and attach it in the instant message along with the geographic details.

- Create a Tasker profile that activates the Jabber Tracker task when entering or leaving a particular geographic location.

- Transmit an instant message whenever the state of the device changes, such as whenever the Bluetooth or WiFi radios turn on or off, when the remaining battery or storage capacity drops below a certain threshold, and when the screen turns on or off.

• Combine the elements of the Jabber Tracker with the segments of the Speak 'n' Tweet project to allow you to send instant messages and post Twitter tweets at the same time.

8.4 Next Steps

In this chapter, we created several practical tasks and scripts that provided us with multiple types of hands-free messaging. We also saw how easy it was to integrate the power of scripting languages like Python with the ease of integrating these scripts with Tasker profiles and tasks. In addition to building upon these projects by enhancing their interactivity or extending their features, we can create new Tasker and SL4A combinations. Consider the following ideas:

• Build your own Google Now or Apple Siri replacement using Android's speech-to-text and text-to-speech capabilities. Customize your intelligent assistant with domain-specific knowledge such as querying sites like Stack Overflow for answers to programming questions.[6]

• Create a geocache recording app that tracks your explorations and exports the tagged map locations to a Keyhole Markup Language (KML)–formatted file for viewing in geographic mapping applications like Google Earth.[7]

• Write a script that obtains your mobile account details, and set up a Tasker task to execute once a day to keep track of your data usage and alert you when you're close to exceeding your mobile data plan.

• Control home automation projects by voice using Tasker tasks and Python or Ruby scripts that send messages to electrified relays and servos connected to Arduinos and Raspberry Pis.[8]

In the next chapter, we are going to take a look at another kind of Android messaging. Specifically, we are going to see how Tasker not only can react to Android notifications but also create them with eye-catching details.

---

6. http://www.stackoverflow.com
7. http://en.wikipedia.org/wiki/Keyhole_Markup_Language
8. http://arduino.cc and http://raspberrypi.org, respectively.

CHAPTER 9

Notification Projects

One of the early innovations that made Android distinct among the various mobile operating systems was its notification tray. Rather than annoy users with modal alert boxes popping up whenever system messages are received, Android neatly organizes these notices into a drop-down list that can be accessed from the upper-left corner of the home screen with the flick of a finger. This approach was so well designed that Apple incorporated the idea into its own iOS mobile operating system.

In this chapter, we will see how we can take Android notifications to a new level with three projects. The first will allow us to selectively convert any notification to speech. This will allow us to continue along the earlier theme of using a headset with Android to keep abreast of all sorts of messaging inputs. The second project will leverage SL4A to grab a very innovative weather-forecasting web service to selectively speak or display the forecast data as a notification. The final project extends Tasker with a plug-in that will allow us to tailor a variety of notification formats for our personal workflow needs. Let's get talking!

9.1   Talking Notifications

Applications that intercept notifications and convert these messages to speech are nothing new. A popular open source program called Voice Notify is a personal favorite.[1] But if you already use Tasker, these types of applications are unnecessary since Tasker offers excellent built-in support for a variety of ways to use and interact with notifications.

This project will essentially replicate entirely in Tasker what programs like Voice Notify can do. We will also use Tasker's built-in regular expression

---

1.   https://play.google.com/store/apps/details?id=com.pilot51.voicenotify

capabilities to filter out notifications that we don't need to hear. Remarkably, we will be able to do all this in just a few simple steps. All we need to do is define a single task and profile for the job.

Tasker's notification events hook into a special type of service on Android used for accessibility purposes. Consequently, you must explicitly allow Tasker to receive these types of events within Android's accessibility settings. Access these settings via the Android Settings application and select the Accessibility menu item. Locate and select the "Tasker - JB" service and set its slider to the On position.

Upon doing so, Android will display a warning that you are explicitly granting Tasker access to any data being entered into the keyboard, screen, and other means of input. Malicious Android applications hooking into this type of service could capture passwords, credit card numbers, and login credentials and send them off to the bad guys without your knowledge. As such, grant access to such sensitive areas only to those programs that you trust with absolute certainty.

After granting Tasker permission to access Android's screen accessibility features, your screen should look like figure shown here.

Now you can call upon Tasker's notification features to capture and create notification events. Let's set up the configuration to do just that.

Tasks and Profiles

Create a new Tasker task by the usual method of selecting the plus icon from the Tasks tab. Name the new task Read Notification. Next, add a single task action by selecting the plus icon within the Task Edit screen. Doing so will display the now familiar Select Action Category dialog. Since we want the task to speak whatever appears in the notification tray, we'll select the now familiar Say action within the Misc action category. This will display the Say Action Edit form.

Choose the tag icon in the Text field to display the Tasker Variable Select pop-up dialog.

Figure 86—Enabling Android accessibility functionality for Tasker

Scroll down and select the Notification Title from the list. This will place the Tasker built-in variable name %NTITLE in the Text field. The Action Edit form should look like Figure 87, *The Action Edit notification form.*

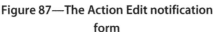

Figure 87—The Action Edit notification form

Figure 88—The Notification Event profile

Save the changes by selecting the Action Edit Say label in the upper-left corner of the screen. Now we need to tell Tasker to run the task whenever a notification is received in Android's notification area. To do so, we need to create a new profile. Select the Profiles tab, followed by the plus icon. Call the new profile Notification and save the name. When the pop-up menu appears, select Event. Within the Event category, choose UI, followed by Notification. Save the changes by selecting the Event Edit Notification label in the upper-left corner. Doing so will display the Tasks pop-up menu. Choose the Read Notification task we created earlier. With the Notification Event profile configured, the Profile screen should look similar to Figure 88, *The Notification Event profile.*

That's all there is to it. Now whenever you receive a text notification in Android's notification area, your device should speak the contents of that message. This comes in handy when using programs such as instant messaging, email, media players, meeting reminders, and news readers that post message updates to the notifications area. If you're already wearing a headset, there's no need to reach for your phone after hearing a notification chime, since Android will read to you whatever message was received.

After the novelty wears off, having Android speak every notification event to you might get annoying and downright aggravating. For instance, whenever SL4A runs a script, it posts a started and exited notification. So if you use the Check Mail script, you will hear not only the results of the script but also that the checkmail.py file has started and exited. That's a lot of chatter. It would be nice if we could filter out unwanted messages from our talking notification task. Thanks to the fact that Tasker supports regular expressions, we can do so. Let's find out how in the next section.

Notification Filter

Tasker's support for regular expressions can be found mainly in its interpretation of conditional statements. In the case of our Read Notification task, we can add a condition to check for a matching pattern in the %NTITLE notification title variable and act on it accordingly. Initially, we want to see whether any part of the %NTITLE string contains a Python file (indicated by the .py extension) followed by SL4A's notification that the Python script has either started or exited.

Building this pattern-matching instruction in a regular expression may look strange if you don't have prior experience building regular expression statements. But once you become familiar with regular expression syntax and experiment with its parsing capabilities, you quickly appreciate the succinct power that is inherent in the technology. Here's the regular expression we will test for in the Read Notification task:

```
/.*\.py\s(started|exited)\.
```

Let's deconstruct the meaning of this statement. The beginning forward slash indicates this is a regular expression statement. The dot, asterisk, backslash, and dot before the py Python file extension tells the parser to accept any character or set of characters leading up to the extension. However, the string being tested must contain the .py literal characters exactly in that order. The \s sequence tells the parser to accept any whitespace character between the .py and the next word in the string. Next, the (started|exited) sequence tells the parser to match the word started or exited after the .py extension. Lastly, since the . (dot) character has a different meaning than just a normal period in regular expression parsing, we need to indicate a period via the escaped sequence (\.) instead. Qualifying matching strings for this regular expression statement would be "MyScript.py started." and "areallylongfilenameforapython-script.py exited." but not "PerlFile.pl started." or "MyPythonScript.py is running."

Add the completed regular expression conditional test to the Read Notification task by editing the Say task and scrolling down until you see the If option. Check the box for the If statement to activate it. Add %NTITLE in the If statement's text edit field as the value to check. Select the conditional operator icon next to it and choose Doesn't Match Regex. This will replace the operator icon with the characters !~R, Tasker's shorthand for not matching a regular expression. Finally, insert the /*.py\s(started|exited)\. expression to test the %NTITLE string against and save the action. Once all the parameters have been set, the Read Notification task assignment should look like the screen shown here:

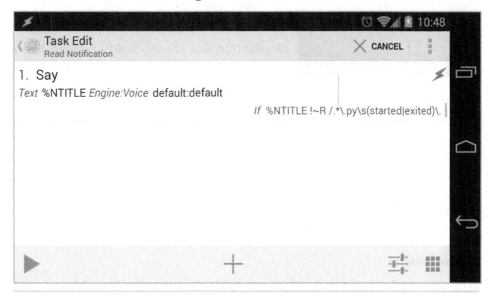

Figure 89—The Read Notification task

Now that the notification filter is in place, you're ready to give Tasker's regular expression parser a test-drive. Execute an SL4A-hosted Python script, such as the checkmail.py script from the Section 8.1, *Check Email*, on page 115, project. If the regular expression condition did its job, you should only hear the spoken results of the checkmail.py script and nothing else. If you hear "checkmail.py started" or "checkmail.py exited," review the conditional regular expression to verify that the syntax is correct.

Figure 90—Show notifications checkbox

Incidentally, besides going through the effort of filtering out specific notifications, you can also opt to disable the display of notifications entirely from a specific application. For example, if we wanted to prevent SL4A from displaying any messages in the notification area, we can go into the application settings via Android settings, select the Apps category, and then select All tab and scroll down to the SL4A program. Selecting it will display an "App info" screen showing how much storage space the application uses, its permissions, and the ability to force stop and uninstall the program. There is also a "Show notifications" checkbox enabled by default, as shown in Figure 90, *Show notifications checkbox.*

Deselecting this checkbox will prevent SL4A from reporting any of its activity, including script starts and stops, in the notification area. While this method will initially accomplish the same objective as our regular expression approach, it is a brute-force technique that we might not want to use. This is because every message from SL4A, regardless of importance, will be prevented from being displayed. Doing so could make debugging and understanding what is happening on your Android a problem. Hence, the more finely tuned regular expression is a better solution overall.

Enhancements

With the regular expression filter, our spoken notification task has allowed us to hear important events without having to look down at our phone or tablet. This includes calendar reminders, instant messaging and SMS posts, system-level notifications, and more. Here are a couple of ideas on how to further enhance these notification events:

- As you become more familiar with the variety of notifications being read, you can decide which ones to filter out and which ones to highlight. Tweak the regular expression to filter out Ruby (*.rb) or Perl (*.pl) scripts if you use those languages instead of Python.

- Check for high-priority events based on the notification text. For example, if you have a critical meeting that you must be reminded about, add a keyword of your choosing to the subject of the meeting. Then add a task that compares that subject string for a keyword match. If a match occurs, use Tasker's Play Ringtone action to bring additional attention to the event. You can further enhance the notification by adding the Notify Vibrate and Notify LED to vibrate and turn on Android's notification light if your hardware supports those features.

- Execute additional scripts or tasks depending on the notifications being received. For example, load your favorite SMS program whenever an SMS notification is received, ready for you to reply to the message as soon as you unlock your screen.

In the next project, we will call upon a really helpful web service to determine a precise near-term weather forecast for our immediate vicinity and post the results to Android's notification area.

9.2   Forecast.io

One of the most useful iPhone programs I've seen is a remarkably accurate weather forecast utility called Dark Sky.[2] Unfortunately, the developers of that program have not ported it to Android. But what they have done is expose their forecast engine as a commercial web service. To help entice developers to incorporate this web service into programs for operating systems other than iOS, the developers offer up to 1,000 free method calls to their Forecast.io service.[3] This is more than enough for our daily needs. Of course, if you plan on using this service beyond this 1,000 method call limit, you can consider additional payment options. But for our single-purpose notification needs, their free limit should be more than enough for now.

Before you can write a script to call the Forecast.io web service, you need to sign up for a free developer account.[4] Upon doing so, you will receive a developer key that you will need to append to your calls to the Forecast.io service. You won't get very far without a key.

Writing the Script

With our developer key in hand, we can write a Python script that will use the GPS coordinates provided by the Tasker %LOC variable just like we did for

---

2.   http://www.darkskyapp.com

3.   http://forecast.io

4.   https://developer.forecast.io/register

the Jabber Tracker project. Then we will combine the latitude and longitude values from the %LOC variable along with the developer key to call to the forecast API. We will then format the response we received from Forecast.io and post the results to Android's notification bar.

While we could work directly with Python's built-in urllib and json modules to unpack the response we received from Forecast.io's servers, there is an easier way. Developer Ze'ev Gilovitz created an easy-to-use Python wrapper for Forecast.io that we'll use for this project. Download the python-forcast.io module from GitHub,[5] and place the uncompressed forecastio.py file (found inside the forecastio folder) into the /sdcard/com.googlecode.pythonforandroid/extras/python folder on your Android device.

With these prerequisites now satisfied, let's take a look at the SL4A Python script and describe each step in detail.

Notifications/forecast.py

```
❶ from forecastio import Forecastio
  import android
  import datetime

  droid = android.Android()

❷ MY_API_KEY = "YOUR_FORECASTIO_DEVELOPER_API_KEY_GOES_HERE"

❸ forecast = Forecastio(MY_API_KEY)
  location = droid.getIntent().result[u'extras'][u'%LOC']

❹ latitude, longitude = location.split(',')
  current_time = datetime.datetime.now()
  response = forecast.loadForecast(latitude,longitude, time=current_time, units="us")

❺ if response['success'] is True:
      Current = forecast.getCurrently()
      Hour = forecast.getHourly()
      result = str(Current.temperature) +
      "F and " + str(Current.summary) + ":" + str(Hour.summary)
      # droid.ttsSpeak(result)
❻     droid.setClipboard(result)
  else:
      droid.setClipboard("There was a problem connecting to the server.")
```

❶ The from keyword is something we haven't seen before in previous SL4A Python programs in this book, but it's simply a way for Python to call upon specific classes in various modules. In this case, we're telling the Python interpreter to reference the Forecastio class within the forecastio

---

5.   https://github.com/ZeevG/python-forcast.io

module. We will be instantiating a Forecastio object shortly. In addition, we will also import the datetime module from Python's standard library and the obligatory Android module for our Android-specific function calls.

❷ This is where you will add your Forecast.io developer API key that was generated for you when you signed up for the service.

❸ On this line, we create a Forecastio object by passing it the developer API key to instantiate the object. Next, we will request the %LOC value from the Tasker script action that we will be creating shortly.

❹ Because the %LOC value combines the latitude and longitude values, we need to separate these into two distinct values to be passed into the forecast object we created earlier. Fortunately, these values are separated by a comma, and Python has a function that makes it easy to assign such known delimited values to distinct variables. In our case, we know that the value of %LOC consists first of the latitude value followed by a comma and then the longitude value. By using the split(',') function, we can separate the two values and assign them to individual latitude and longitude variables accordingly.

In addition to latitude and longitude, we need one more important piece of data to pass to the loadforecast function, that being the time we want the forecast data to reflect. In addition to current forecast data, Forecast.io also offers historical weather data for analysis. However, since we're interested in the current weather and forecast conditions, we will pass the current time by calling upon Python's datetime.datetime.now() function. With our latitude, longitude, and forecast time values in hand, we can submit our request to the Forecast.io web service. Note that we can also specify the type of measurement units we would like Forecast.io to return to us so we don't have to perform our own temperature conversions on the fly. In this case, we are assigning units="us" for temperature values to be returned in degrees Fahrenheit.

❺ Assuming we have received an acceptable response from the Forecast.io web service, we can then parse the response data for the current temperature and day's forecast summary. Convert these responses to a string and format it for placement into the notification area. Note the inclusion of the colon in the string. This is done so we can place the current temperature and weather condition in a notification title and the day's forecast into the notification body. We will use this inserted colon later as a delimiter for Tasker to split the string into title and body portions.

Also note the call to the droid.ttsSpeak() function that has been commented out. You can uncomment this if you want to hear the forecast summary spoken to you right away, or you can use it in place of the notification altogether. I found it helpful to uncomment while testing and then, depending on my needs, comment it out if I choose to have the Talking Notifications project we created earlier running. After all, if the Talking Notifications is active and the droid.ttsSpeak() line is uncommented, we will hear the current weather conditions spoken twice.

❻ This last line is used as a hack to get around an annoying limitation. While Tasker is perfectly capable of passing parameters to SL4A running Python, doing the reverse isn't supported. What Tasker does support is the ability to read and assign the contents of Android's clipboard to a Tasker variable. That's why we're copying the results of our concatenated weather forecast string into the clipboard.

While you will see how this works when we create the Tasker task for this project, you may have also correctly surmised that using the clipboard for this purpose isn't the most elegant way to handle the passing of variables from a script's output to a Tasker variable. While its occurrence is rare, you may see the forecast notification show the contents of the last text copy operation if such an action was performed while the script was running. But it's what we have to work with until Tasker's creator can provide a more elegant format for accepting passed values.

After you have entered the script, save it to a file called localforecast.py by selecting Android's back button. Once the file is saved, we can configure Tasker to call the localforecast.py Python script.

Tasker Integration

Just as we did earlier with the Jabber Tracker project, we will pass the latitude and longitude values that Tasker captured and supply them to the localforecast.py Python script for processing. After this script has executed, we will then have Tasker incorporate the forecast results that were copied to Android's clipboard into the notification output.

We will start by creating a new task called Forecast.io. Normally, the first action in this new task would have been to turn on the GPS radio so we could capture the current latitude and longitude coordinates. But as we discovered previously in the Section 8.3, *Jabber Tracker*, on page 136, project, the auto-mated GPS On/Off functionality works only on older or rooted Android devices.

Therefore, to have this task execute properly, we will need to make sure to manually turn on the GPS radio before the Forecast.io task is run.

With that in mind, the first step in our Forecast.io task will be to add a Get Location action via Tasker's Misc Action category. You can alter the GPS signal acquisition timeout value, but the default setting of 100 seconds is typically enough for most purposes. Leave everything else on this action to the default values. This includes leaving the Continue Task Immediately and Continue Task After Error settings both unchecked. After all, we need the current location information to pass to the localforecast.py script. We also don't want to execute the rest of the task if we fail to obtain this vital GPS information.

Following a successful GPS coordinate lock-on, we can proceed to run the localforecast.py SL4A script. Add this by selecting the plus icon in the middle of the lower Task toolbar and choose Script followed by the Run SL4A Script action. Assign the Name field of this action to the localforecast.py file. Add the %LOC location variable to the Pass Variables field and save the action. That takes care of providing the script with latitude and longitude data and executing the Python script.

Next, we have to assign the contents of the Android clipboard that contains the copy of the script's results to a Tasker variable. To do so, create a new Tasker variable called %FORECASTIO and set it equal to the contents of the clipboard. Tasker's built-in variable name for the clipboard is %CLIP. Thus, add a new action to the task and select the Variables action category followed by the Variable Set action. In the Name field, enter the new %FORECASTIO variable name. In the To field, enter the built-in %CLIP variable.

But there's a problem. If we ran this action immediately following the Run SL4A Script action, we wouldn't see the correct results being assigned to the %FORECASTIO variable. That's because Tasker doesn't wait for the localforecast.py to finish executing. Instead, it runs the next action immediately, so whatever happens to be in the Android clipboard at the time is what gets assigned to the %FORECASTIO variable. To fix this, we need to tell Tasker to wait a few seconds before running the next action to give enough time for the Forecast.io server to respond.

In between the Run SL4A Script action and the Variable Set action, add a new action that will tell Tasker to wait for several seconds. Five seconds seems to work for me, but your delay needs may vary based on network speeds and your device's processing and resource constraints. Select the Wait action from the Task action category. In the Wait Action Edit screen, set the Seconds value to 5 or more, depending on your needs. Save the changes.

Recall how we added the colon character to the following line in our Python script:

```
result = str(Current.temperature) +
"F and " + str(Current.summary) + ":" + str(Hour.summary)
```

It's time to put that delimiting colon character to use. We are going to use Tasker's Variable Split action as we did earlier in the Talking Clock task, but instead of splitting on a period, we're going to split on the colon character instead. Add the action via the Variables category followed by the Variable Split action. In the Name field, add the %FORECASTIO variable. In the Splitter field, add the colon (:) character. Recall from the Talking Clock task that the Variable Split action will split the results of the task into consecutively named variables from the root variable named in the Variable Split Name field. In our case, this action will generate two new variables, %FORECASTIO1 and %FORECASTIO2.

Now take these two newly generated variables and assign them to a new notification notice. Add a Notify action from the Alert action category. In the Title field, add the %FORECASTIO1 variable. In the Text field, add the %FORECASTIO2 variable. You can also add a custom icon to accompany the notification if you want, just as I have done in Figure 91, *The Action Edit dialog*.

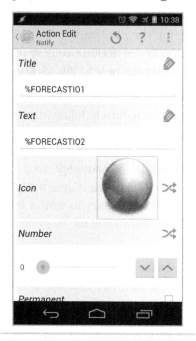

Figure 91—The Action Edit dialog

Figure 92—The complete Forecast.io task

Save the Notify action. Your Forecast.io task is now complete, and the task definition should look like the one shown in Figure 92, *The complete Forecast.io task*, on page 156.

Testing the Weather

We're ready to take it for a test run. Since this task is so heavily dependent on your current geographic coordinates, turning on and ensuring that your GPS radio has a lock on the GPS satellites is vital. Once the GPS radio is activated, verify that your location is accurately reported in Google Maps. Then make sure you have an active Internet connection and run the task within Tasker. You can also create a Task widget to make accessing the Forecast.io task easier from the Android home screen, as we have done with previous projects.

If your run was successful, you should see a notification appear. Pull the notification tray down to view both the notification title and the body text. It should look something like Figure 93, *A Forecast.io notification*. Depending on the length of the body text, you may notice that the text doesn't wrap if it exceeds the length of the notification pull-down tray. See the example in Figure 94, *The notification text field length exceeded*.

Figure 93—A Forecast.io notification

Figure 94—The notification text field length exceeded

Unfortunately, this text overflow issue is a limitation in the current version of Tasker. Prior releases of the Android OS limited text lengths to the width of the notification area. With the release of Android OS versions 4.1 and newer, notification text can now be programmed to wrap around and accommodate longer messages in the text field. You have likely noticed this with the display of email and SMS notifications. Tasker hasn't yet adopted this new OS feature, but it's on the developer's to-do list. In the meantime, is there anything we can do to fix this? As a matter of fact there is, but we need some outside assistance to make it happen. That's what we will explore in the next project.

Enhancements

I have found in my projects that the most effective use of the notification area is for semi-persistent messages, such as meeting reminders, instant messages, and important system state changes. Be cautious with using notifications too frequently, since you will quickly become desensitized to them and they lose their effectiveness. With that in mind, here are a couple ideas that can benefit from employing notifications:

- Revisit earlier projects in the book and retrofit them with an option to use notifications. For example, adding notifiers to the Tasker Pomodoro widget could enhance the widget's end alarm, as well as provide a timestamp of when the Pomodoro session began and ended.

- For more complex tasks that take a long time to complete, posting a notification when the task is done will go a long way toward keeping you informed of the status of automated processes on your device.

- Incorporate push notification services like Google Cloud Services (GCM) for Android or third-party services like Pushover to keep track of events from other people and machines.[6]

In the next project, we're going to not only correct the text autowrap limitation in the Forecast.io project but also learn how to incorporate Tasker plug-ins to further enhance ease-of-use automation control over our devices.

9.3   AutoNotification

One of the best, most forward-thinking features of Tasker is its ability to be extended via third-party plug-ins. These plug-ins are available in the Google Play store as dedicated Tasker add-ons, or they can be occasionally incorporated into Android programs. The Headset Button Controller program, for

---

6.   http://developer.android.com/google/gcm/index.html or https://pushover.net, respectively.

instance, includes a Tasker plug-in that allows you to automatically select a headset profile to use. For example, you could have a Tasker profile that detects when you have entered or left your home and change to a different headset profile using a different set of assigned button presses as a result.

In the case of notifications, a really useful plug-in has been created by prolific Tasker plug-in developer João Dias. His AutoNotification Tasker plug-in gives you an easy way to access, format, and manipulate Android notifications.[7]

In addition to AutoNotification, João has created several other compelling Tasker plug-ins.[8] One of these is called AutoRemote.[9] This plug-in allows you to send messages to and from your Android device and other smartphones or computers like those running Windows, OS X, or Linux. This greatly extends your smartphone or tablet's participation in a much wider workflow. But for now, let's install the AutoNotification plug-in and take a closer look at what it has to offer. We'll also use it to fix the word-wrap problem we discovered using the standard Tasker notification action in the Forecast.io project.

Installing Tasker Plug-ins

AutoNotification is available from the Google Play store initially as a free, albeit limited, plug-in. The free version allows you to try it before you buy the in-app purchase that removes constraints on text message size and profile names. The commercial version also offers the ability to change LED color and blink duration along with vibration and custom sound effect support. Note that some of the features of the plug-in, such as the expanded multiline notification text option, are available only on devices running Android 4.2 or newer. Thus, the following example won't work on devices running older versions of the Android OS.

Let's try it in Tasker by creating a new task called AutoNotify Test. Then add a new action via the plus icon in the middle of the lower Tasker toolbar. Select the Plugin Action Category followed by the AutoNotification action, as shown in Figure 95, *The Notify Action Edit dialog*, on page 160.

Select the Edit button in the Configuration Action Edit setting. Doing so will open AutoNotification's Share Options dialog, as shown in Figure 96, *AutoNotification share options*, on page 160. This is where the genius of this plug-in shines. Nearly every facet of Android's notification properties can be configured in this screen. These include the usual title and text that we're

---

7.   https://play.google.com/store/apps/details?id=com.joaomgcd.autonotification

8.   https://play.google.com/store/search?q=joaomgcd&c=apps

9.   https://play.google.com/store/apps/details?id=com.joaomgcd.autoremote

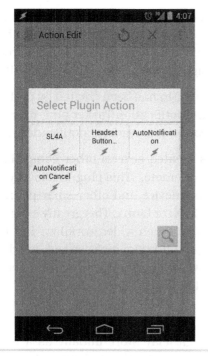

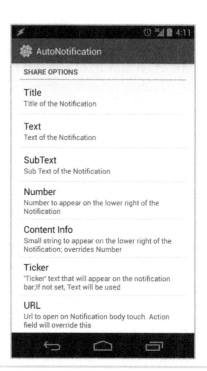

Figure 95—The Notify Action Edit dialog   **Figure 96—AutoNotification share options**

already familiar with in Tasker, as well as more exotic settings such as subtext, ticker text, notification persistence, picture, vibration patterns, progress bars, and more.

We will create a test notification to see how some of these custom settings are rendered. Set the title of the notification to AutoNotification Test. Set the text to "The AutoNotification plug-in is pretty cool and extends notifications in many different ways." Set SubText equal to "I need to learn more about this plug-in." Lastly, scroll down and check the Share option. This will allow the content of the notification to be shared with other Android applications via a Share option that will appear below the notification text. Save the changes and run the task. Pull down the notification bar to reveal the generated notification, which should look similar to the one shown in Figure 97, *AutoNotification example*, on page 161.

That looks much better than the standard notification text. It matches the kind of feature-rich polish that you might see in high-end Android programs. Using this newfound enhanced ability, we can revisit the notification feature in the Forecast.io project to properly format overflowing text.

Word Wrap Repair

Reopen the Forecast.io task and remove the Notify action by long-pressing the action until the Tasker toolbar is at the top of the screen. The toolbar allows only selected tasks to be cut or copied. Cutting an action or task is essentially the same thing as deleting one, assuming you replace or clear Android's copy buffer with other contents. So, in this case, choose the Cut icon (the one that looks like scissors lying on a sheet of paper). Doing so removes the Notify action from the Forecast.io task.

Now replace the cut Notify task with one that calls the AutoNotification plug-in. Select the plus icon in the lower toolbar and select the Plugin Action Category. From there, choose the AutoNotification Plugin Action and select the Edit button to the right of the Configuration label. Enter the %FORECASTIO0 variable in the Title field. In the Text field, enter the %FORECASTIO1 variable. Then in the SubText field, enter the phrase "Select for Weather Map."

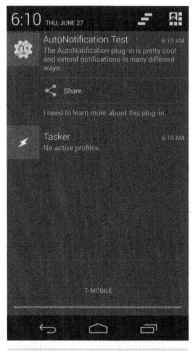

Figure 97—AutoNotification example

Finally in the URL field, enter the URL of the weather map in your area. Since I live in the United States, I chose to use radar maps made available from Accuweather.com.[10] Enter your city and state in Accuweather's search box. From the weather overview for your city, select the Radar tab followed by the More Radar & Maps hyperlink. Doing so will show a static image of your state radar map. Depending on your browser, you should be able to right-click (or in the case of a Mac, control-click) the radar map and copy the image address. This will provide a static URL where this frequently updated radar image resides. In my case, Accuweather

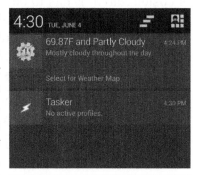

Figure 98—The revised AutoNotification action for Forecast.io

---

10. http://www.accuweather.com

served up a GIF image of the radar overview with the filename INMREIL_.gif.[11] With these parameters set, the AutoNotification Action Edit screen should look like the one in Figure 98, *The revised AutoNotification action for Forecast.io*, on page 161.

Running the Forecast.io task generates an AutoNotification-styled Android notification complete with the weather map link. Since we didn't choose an icon to use for the notification, AutoNotification substituted the default Tasker icon for us instead. AutoNotification not only allows us to change this icon but also add an icon in the notification message. And check out how

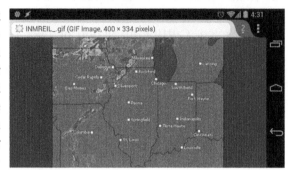

Figure 99—Selecting the notification displays the weather map in a web browser.

choosing the "Select for Weather Map" SubText opens a web browser showing the weather map at the time the Forecast.io task was last executed, like the one shown here.

Enhancements

We have scratched the surface of what AutoNotification can do and the degree of customization it has to offer. Because there are so many ideas, layouts, formats, and other options within this extensive plug-in, spend time exploring it and tinkering with the settings. As you become more familiar with it, you will quickly realize new possibilities of how to apply it to your own Android notification needs. Here are just a few enhancements worth exploring further:

- Include a routine in the Forecast.io script that properly sets the weather map URL for the appropriate region of the captured GPS coordinates.

- Include an image file fetching routine in the Forecast.io Python script for the weather radar map. Reference the weather map image in AutoNotification's Picture field and display it along with the rest of the retrieved forecast text.

- Create a Tasker profile that runs the modified Forecast.io task at set time intervals or whenever you travel into or out of a defined geographic region.

---

11. http://sirocco.accuweather.com/nx_mosaic_400x300c/RE/INMREIL_.gif

- Make the Forecast.io notification persistent so that you don't have to keep clearing the notification each time you review the notification bar. This advantage will become even more apparent after you set up the time-based event profile for the task.

9.4   Next Steps

The Android notification area plays an important role in managing real-time inbound information and helps keep you informed without cluttering your screen with annoying pop-up messages. Skilled user interface designers and developers make this look obvious and effortless in elegant Android applications, but it takes practice coupled with a lot of trial and error to see what works and what doesn't. That's why I find working with Tasker's notification functionality coupled with plug-ins like AutoNotification to be so helpful. If something doesn't look quite right, I can immediately jump into the task and tweak the settings until the results are satisfying.

Using this approach, consider other uses for pouring the results of your own programs, scripts, and tasks into the notification bar, such as the following:

- Enhance the Pomodoro widget with time-stamped start and stop notifications. When selecting the stop notification, open a Pomodoro log file that prepopulates the entry with your start and stop time and allows you to enter additional notes, completed tasks, or other measures of productivity success completed within that duration.

- Create a task that executes additional scripts upon receiving text in a notification that matches a defined string. For example, if the string contains the SMS name, phone number, or other unique identifier of your partner, set the phone to a unique vibrate pattern and/or audio cue until the notification bar is accessed.

- Make your own pull-down system stats notification area showing remaining battery charge, GPS coordinates, and radio on/off status in a static or ticker-style format.

In the next chapter, we are going to explore projects that incorporate graphic user interface elements. Doing so will demonstrate how Tasker and SL4A can be used to create applications that rival native graphic application functionality. We will also further extend Tasker with additional plug-ins to help us realize these project possibilities faster than ever before.

CHAPTER 10

Graphics Projects

Nearly all the projects in this book leading up to this chapter have been focused on audio-oriented, hands-free operation. While that satisfies a great deal of useful tasks, especially when you're constantly on the go, sometimes a picture truly speaks a thousand words.

In this chapter, we're going to take a look at a couple of projects that work best with a user interface. We will learn about the graphic user interface (GUI) designer that is bundled with Tasker. We'll create the interface elements and wire those up with tasks that execute when those onscreen elements are interacted with.

Let's start with a simple yet essential visual application that will help us get used to the GUI tools while at the same time producing a toolbar that can be built upon with our own expanding library of Tasker tasks and GUI-based programs.

10.1 Application Launcher

The Application Launcher will provide us with a row of icons that will be displayed onscreen. We can launch this application either via a Tasker widget or, the way I prefer, using a gesture courtesy of Nova Launcher Prime's gesture assignment options. The icon toolbar features icons assigned to run some of the projects we have created in earlier chapters. As our task library grows, we can use this custom icon-centric app-launching program to help organize and categorize the expanding variety of custom tasks we build.

To get started, we are going to use Tasker's Scene Designer to build the user interface and create a layout to place task-centric icons. Using the icons that were assigned earlier to each task, we can first draw a rectangle that will serve as the surface where the icons will be placed. Touching the appropriate icon will launch the associated task or program.

Creating a Scene

Tasker scene elements essentially act as containers for other scene elements or Tasker actions. For example, a button selection can be assigned to run a task. In the case of our application launcher, we will use the Perform Task function and assign various tasks to be run (such as running the Talking Clock task for one of our app launcher buttons).

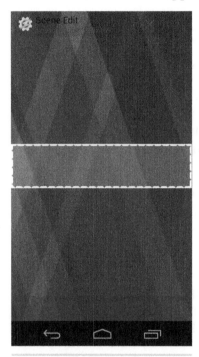

While we could create a series of freestanding buttons for each task or program we want to run, it will be easier to organize and nicer-looking if we place these buttons into a rectangular frame. To do so, select the Scenes tab in Tasker and create a new scene via the plus icon. Name the scene App Launcher. Tasker will then show a blank screen with a center rectangle. This is the scene container. You can resize the container by long-pressing the container and moving your finger left, right, up, or down to alter its width and height. Set the width and height roughly to the size of a Tasker task icon, as shown in the figure here.

Once you're satisfied with the container's dimensions, you can save your changes by selecting the back button or the Tasker icon in the upper-left corner of the screen. Then reselect the scene to continue editing it.

Figure 100—The App Launcher scene container

Now that we have a container to house our task program icons, we can begin adding tasks in the form of buttons. You can assign different actions to buttons depending on whether the button graphic registers a tap or long-tap event. For our app launcher, we will use the same single-tap event to run the Perform task for each of the tasks we have chosen to include in the launcher container. To add a new button, press and hold your finger within the container. This will pop up an element menu, allowing you to select from a variety of graphic elements, as shown in Figure 101, *A selection of scene elements*, on page 167.

When you create a button for our app launcher toolbar, it will initially display the UI tab for that element. This is where you can set the size, background color, icon, and position. For example, let's add the Talking Clock launch

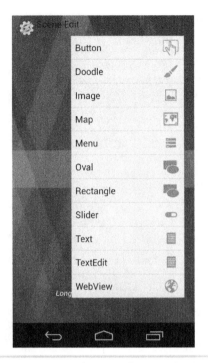

Figure 101—A selection of scene elements

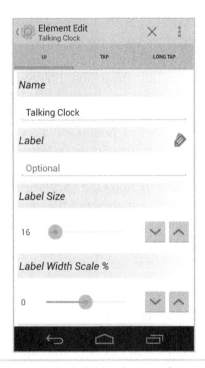

Figure 102—Editing a button element

action to our toolbar. Leave the default UI values and select an icon to visually represent the task. For the Talking Clock, I chose the same icon as the one I assigned previously to the Talking Clock task. (See Figure 102, *Editing a button element*.)

With the look defined, we need to assign an action to perform when the button is selected. Choose the TAP tab and add a new action by selecting the plus icon. Since we want to run the Talking Clock task, choose the Task category followed by the Perform Task action. In the Name field, select the magnifying glass icon to select the Talking Clock task.

Continue populating the app launcher container with other buttons and assign them the appropriate tasks. In my case, I chose to populate my app launcher with the Talking Clock, Check Email, Forecast.io, Jabber Tracker, and Speak 'n' Tweet tasks, as shown in Figure 103, *The fully populated app launcher*, on page 168.

You will also notice I created a button with an X character to represent a close toolbar button action. I chose to create my own custom close button so that I didn't have to rely on Tasker's built-in close scene button size.

For our custom close scene button to work, we need to select it just as we did with our other app launcher buttons and assign it an action to hide the toolbar (in other words, the scene). Do so by choosing the TAP tab and adding a new action. Select the Scene action from the Select Action Category screen, followed by the Hide Scene Action option. Tasker should autopopulate the scene Name field for you with our App Launcher scene name, but if it doesn't, simply select the magnifying glass and choose it from the Select Scene pop-up listing. (See Figure 103, *The fully populated app launcher*)

Building the Task

With our custom close button action assigned, our toolbar is complete. But we still need to create a Tasker task to initially display our App Launcher toolbar. Select the Task tab in Tasker and create a new task called App Launcher. Create a new action and choose

Figure 103—The fully populated app launcher

the Scene category. Then select the Show Scene action. Select the magnifying glass in the Name field of the Show Scene dialog and select the App Launcher scene from the pop-up list.

Next, select the Display As drop-down list box and take a moment to review the number of display combinations Tasker can apply to scenes. These range from full windows to dialogs to overlays. Because we want to display our application launcher as a toolbar that overlays on top of our home screen as well as grab input focus to capture touch events, choose the Overlay, Blocking display style.

Moving on to the Horizontal and Vertical position settings, you can choose wherever you like to place the overlay toolbar on the screen. In my case, I prefer the top center of the screen. So, that means setting the Horizontal Position slider to Centre and the Vertical Position slider to Up. Finally, deselect the Show Exit Button setting, since we previously created our own exit button on the form. Note that when you do so, Tasker will warn you with a reminder that you will have to manage the closing action and hiding of the forms yourself (see Figure 104, *Exit button warning for overlay scenes*, on page 169).

Save the action by selecting the Action Edit Show Scene label in the upper-left corner of the screen. Your App Launcher task should look similar to Figure 105, *The App Launcher task*, on page 170.

You can test your handiwork by running the App Launcher task. Doing so, you should see your App Launcher scene display in the upper center of the screen. Touching any of the application icons should launch the appropriately assigned program. You should also be able to hide the scene by selecting the X button that we assigned to hide the scene.

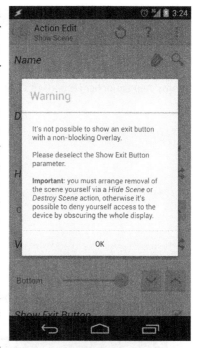

Figure 104—Exit button warning for overlay scenes

Assigning a Gesture

Now that you have a working application launcher task, we need an easy way to invoke it. While we could create a widget icon to reference the task and launch our App Launcher task when we select that widget, it would be more elegant if we could instantiate it with a simple two-finger swipe up on the home screen. Thanks to Nova Launcher Prime (*Nova Launcher Prime*, on page 12), assigning gestures like this to tasks or programs is a simple affair.

Access the Nova Launcher Prime settings screen via the Nova Settings app icon in the Android applications screen. From there, select the Gestures and Buttons category. This screen allows you to reassign the gesture behaviors for several popular home screen gestures, such as pinching in and out and swiping up or down using one or two fingers, as you can see in Figure 106, *Nova Launcher Prime gesture settings*, on page 170.

Select the Swipe up (Two Fingers) item. Nova Launcher will ask you to assign an action to this gesture. Select the Shortcuts tab and scroll down to the Task Shortcut. Selecting the Task Shortcut item will display a list of Tasker tasks. Choose the App Launcher task and save the changes. If everything has been correctly configured, you should be able to swipe up on the home screen with two fingers, and the App Launcher should display in the top of the screen, as shown in Figure 107, *The final running Application Launcher*, on page 170.

Figure 105—The App Launcher task

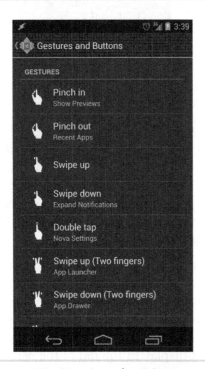

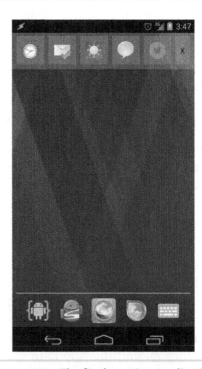

Figure 106—Nova Launcher Prime gesture settings

Figure 107—The final running Application Launcher

Depending on what kind of desktop background you use or the number of icons on your home screen, the translucent nature of the App Launcher's background may make it difficult to see and select the launch icons. If that turns out to be the case, edit the App Launcher scene and change the background from its current semitransparent value to a more solid color. You can do this by selecting the Background Colour menu option from the Scene Edit menu, as shown in the next figure.

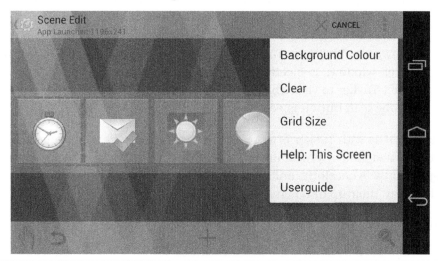

Figure 108—Scene Edit menu

Feel free to alter the size of the icons to increase their touch target areas or make them smaller to fit more icons in a single row. You can also enhance the application launcher in several useful ways to make it more than just a toolbar of shortcuts.

Enhancements

Since this is our first foray into the ability to construct graphic user interfaces for our Tasker (and even SL4A) tasks, the App Launcher project offers a useful starter template to build upon. It can also be used as a timesaving sandbox to play with new ideas, since the basic interface and display rules have already been created. You can extend the application launcher's functionality with the following ideas:

- Replace toolbar icons based on the current state. For example, if you have a toggle to turn on and off the Bluetooth or WiFi radios, display the appropriate icon to show whether the radio is active.

- Take a minimal clutter approach to the home screen by removing all icons and widgets and place only your most popular apps on the App Launcher toolbar. In addition to befuddling others with your strikingly empty screen, there is also a mild "security through obscurity" benefit because only you know the correct gesture to access the launch targets for your favorite Android programs, scripts, and tasks.

- Turn the application launcher into a full-blown web browser that overlays on top of the home screen whenever you need to quickly refer to a web page. Extend the background frame to host a TextEdit Tasker component along with a WebView Tasker component for the web URL entry and browser window, respectively. Create a button with a globe icon and instruct Tasker to visit whatever URL is in the TextEdit component when the globe icon button is selected.

Creating GUIs with Tasker is a breeze once you get used to the basic drawing and task assignment procedures. We will build upon these skills in the next project that will check the online status of several Internet-accessible servers and display their up or down status in a Tasker screen.

10.2 Twitch.tv Widget

Before pursuing a full-time technology career more than fifteen years ago, I was a magazine editor of both a computer and a videogaming magazine. Even though I don't have the time to dedicate to electronic gaming, I still enjoy both watching and playing with skilled gamers (with my son being my favorite gaming opponent and mentor). One streaming media service that taps into this joy of sharing gaming strategies is Twitch.tv.[1] The service was also chosen by Microsoft to be a premier game broadcast provider for the Xbox One gaming console, though Twitch.tv accepts game streams from all the major platforms, including Sony's PlayStation 3, PCs, and even Android and iOS devices. If you haven't seen Twitch.tv streams, head over to the site and take a look at the various live channels broadcasting dozens of different games twenty-four hours a day. Note that while creating a free account allows you to follow favorite users on the service, it's not mandatory that you have an account to check on user status and watch broadcasts.

Twitch.tv released an Android client to log into and view its services (you can obtain the free Twitch.tv application from the Play store[2]), but it's not as feature-rich as its iOS counterpart. Besides lacking a built-in live chat client

---

1. http://twitch.tv
2. https://play.google.com/store/apps/details?id=tv.twitch.android.viewer

and having occasional bugs, Twitch.tv for Android lacks a key feature that could make it stand out above any feature on other platforms. Specifically, having a Twitch.tv widget that shows the current broadcast status of favorite gaming broadcasters would be far more helpful than digging for that information in the full application. Fortunately, using Tasker, JavaScript, the Twitch.tv web API, and a widget-building toolkit called Zoom, we can create our own Twitch.tv broadcast status widget.

Using JavaScript

Like the web service project in Section 9.2, *Forecast.io*, on page 151, the web API for Twitch.tv returns JavaScript Object Notation (JSON)–formatted results. And while we certainly could use the same Python-scripted SL4A approach for this project that we used for the Forecast project, we're going to use Tasker's built-in support for JavaScript instead. In addition to the features available for Android's browser-based JavaScript engine, Tasker has added a number of JavaScript functions of its own to provide more extensive interoperability with Tasker's capabilities.[3]

Tasker offers two options for working with JavaScript code. The first is similar to SL4A by accessing, parsing, and interpreting an external script file. The second more interesting option is embedding the script within a Tasker task. Tasker calls this a JavaScriptlet, and that's the approach we are going to take with this project. While there's no discernible performance improvement using JavaScriptlets over external .js files, the benefit of packaging tasks into a single dependency is to make it more manageable, since everything you need is located in the same place within the same program. More importantly, the JavaScript interpreter supported by Android includes a full JSON stack, exactly what we will need to decode the results of the Twitch.tv web API call.

Constructing the Task

The task we'll build for this project is straightforward. We will essentially make an HTTP GET web request to Twitch.tv's API, parse the JSON results that are returned, format the data for rich-text output, and post the text to a text area within a widget. We'll also create a username variable that can be easily modified and passed to the web request URL string. So let's start with that step and move forward.

Create a new task in Tasker and name it Twitch Channel. Create a new variable called %CHANNEL by selecting Variable Set from the Variables Action

---

3. http://tasker.dinglisch.net/userguide/en/javascript.html

category. In the NAME field, enter the variable name %CHANNEL. In the To field, enter the username of a Twitch.tv user you enjoy following. For this example, I am going to set the username to one of my favorite Twitch.tv broadcasters known as Dan's Gaming. Dan employs a clever green-screen effect on his broadcasts that allows viewers to see him speak comments and see his reactions to onscreen events. He is also a passionate gamer who makes clever, often funny, and insightful comments about his entertaining gaming adventures. His Twitch.tv username is dansgaming.

With the %CHANNEL variable assigned, our next step will be to create an HTTP Get action from the Net action category. This is where we will call the Twitch.tv API for user channel broadcast status and pass our %CHANNEL variable into the URL request. For the Server:Port value, enter the URL https://api.twitch.tv/kraken/streams/%CHANNEL. If you're curious about learning what this and other Twitch.tv web service URLs can provide, visit Twitch.tv's GitHub page for more details about the Twitch.tv web API.[4]

The default global variable that Tasker assigns to and stores the results of an HTTP Get request is called HTTPD. This is the variable we will access in our JavaScriptlet to retrieve channel details, such as the title of the stream being broadcast as well as the number of people currently watching the stream. Create a JavaScriptlet action from the Script action category. In the Code field, enter the following JavaScript:

Graphics/twitch.js
```
❶ var channelDetails = JSON.parse(global('HTTPD'));
  var info = "";

  try {
❷     info = channelDetails['stream']['channel']['status'];
❸     info += " <b><font color='green'>(";
      info += channelDetails['stream']['viewers'];
      info += ")</font></b>";
❹ } catch(error) {
      info = "<font color='red'>" + global('CHANNEL') + " unavailable.</font>";
  }

❺ setGlobal('TWITCHRESULT', info);
```

Let's take a closer look at what this code does.

❶ We create a variable called channelDetails and run JavaScript's JSON.Parse function on the %HTTPD global variable that we created from the prior Tasker HTTP Get action. We also initialize an empty string variable called

---

4. https://github.com/justintv/Twitch-API

info that will be used to build the HTML-rich text string to be displayed in our widget's text area.

❷ Within a try/catch block, we begin by interrogating the JSON-parsed channelDetails object and query the value of the ['stream']['channel']['status'] channel status. Then we assign the channel status results to our info string. We will append more text to this info string later via the += operator.

❸ We continue to build the info string with HTML formatting (setting the name of the channel in the color green), since we will place the results of info into a text area that interprets and renders HTML markup. This will give our final text string more presentation polish and help us visually identify different details being displayed in the combined info string. We also query the value of channelDetails again, this time requesting the number of people watching the currently broadcasting stream via the ['stream']['viewers'] value. Then we conclude the info string with closing font and bold tags.

❹ In the event that we encounter an error retrieving the channel status and stream viewers values, we need to alert the widget with an error. The most likely reason for this error is that the chosen username is not broadcasting and therefore does not return any values for those two fields. The other possibility is a problem connecting to the network to query the Twitch.tv web API. Either way, the channel status is unavailable and we need to report it as such. Wrapping the results in a red font color will help it stand out even more.

❺ Lastly, regardless of whether the user is broadcasting, we need to place the concatenated string of the info variable into a Tasker variable that we can pass along to other Tasker-connected task assignments, such as the contents of a text field within a custom widget.

The last step we need to do to complete the task is place the contents of the compiled %TWITCHRESULT global variable into a text field on a custom widget. But before we can do that, we need to create the custom widget user interface and name the elements of the user interface. It is via these names that we will be able to access and assign the user interface elements text properties.

But unlike the application launcher project, we can't use scenes to create a widget. That is because a widget is a fixture on the home screen, and widgets can be embedded in selected areas of individual home-screen pages. Conversely, a Tasker scene is an overlay that stays in a fixed location on the screen. It doesn't give you the option of embedding the user interface the way a widget does. Fortunately, the makers of Tasker addressed this limitation by creating a free Android utility that solves this problem.

Zooming Along

Zoom, developed by Crafty Apps EU (the same people who created Tasker), is a free widget construction utility available from the Google Play store.[5] It can be used to make widgets with buttons, images, text, and other graphics. Better yet, each of these elements can be accessed and modified by Tasker actions. So in the case of our Twitch.tv channel widget, we can create a user interface in Zoom and assign the main text field the contents of the %TWITCHRESULT variable.

Building a widget user interface using Zoom is similar to building Tasker scenes, though Zoom does have a few quirks of its own. One of these annoyances is how Zoom rarely renders a widget UI the way you designed it. Because of various factors such as different Android hardware devices with different screen dimensions, calibrations, and font metrics, it's just one of those design aspects that you will have to tweak to get the widget's graphic and text elements to look just right.

Once Zoom has been installed from the Google Play store, launch it and create a new widget template by selecting the green plus arrow in the lower-right corner. Name the template Twitch Channel and assign it a cell width and height of 2 x 1. Zoom will warn you that the dimension chosen won't be able to create the widget with those dimensions. However, because Zoom was created prior to the changes made to the way widgets can be displayed and resized on the fly in Android 4.2 and newer, this warning is no longer relevant. As for the other settings, you can leave the default values in place, as shown in the figure here.

Figure 109—Twitch Widget Zoom template properties

Select the green check mark icon in the lower left of the Template Properties screen to save the changes. You will then be asked to name the template. Name the template Twitch Channel. Then you will be taken to the design screen. You

---

5. https://play.google.com/store/apps/details?id=net.dinglisch.android.zoom

can add various graphic items to the layout by long-touching the screen, keeping the graphic items within the white margin of the widget. Doing so will pop up the New Element Type dialog, where you can choose to add buttons, images, text elements, and more to the screen. For the Twitch widget, we will need two text elements, one for the title and one for the body text of the widget.

Create the first text element by long-pressing the design screen and selecting Text from the New Element Type dialog. This will display the various properties that can be set for the text element. Since this will be the element we will use to show the title of our widget, call the element Broadcast Status. Set the Text property to Broadcast Status as well. Text elements can be formatted either as Standard Text or as HTML. HTML is useful when you want to alter the various characters displayed in the text element with different font styles, sizes, and colors. But since our title text is going to be consistently the same color and size, we can keep the format in Standard Text. Then you can set the Text Colour, Text Size, Text Scale Width, and Center attributes of the text. You can set these attributes to whatever works for your screen size. For my Galaxy Nexus, I chose the text size equal to 22 and the text scale width equal to 0.75. For text color, either enter the HTML color code equivalent or select the magnifying glass icon to choose the color from a color wheel and slider. Lastly, the Click Action property represents the action that Zoom should take when the text element is selected within the working widget. Select the magnifying glass icon to display the Action Type dialog. Scroll down to find and select the Tasker task. This will display the Task Selection dialog. Find the Twitch Channel task we created earlier and select it. This way, we can manually run the Twitch Channel task whenever we select the Broadcast Status title text in the widget. When done, the Broadcast Status property screen should look similar to Figure 110, *Broadcast Text properties*, on page 178.

Add a second text element as a container for the %TWITCHRESULT variable result from running the Twitch Channel task. Set the Element Name and Text property fields to Status. Because we want to render the HTML code in the %TWITCHRESULT result, set the Format field to HTML. And like the Broadcast Status text field, change the Text Colour, Size, and Scale Width to what best suits your particular device. For my Galaxy Nexus, I set the text color to white (#FFFFFFFF), size to 12, and scale width to 1.0. As for the Click Action setting, select the magnifying glass icon and choose Launch App from the Action Type dialog. Assuming you have already installed the Twitch.tv client for Android, scroll down until you find and then select the Twitch program. Once set, your

Figure 110—Broadcast Text properties

Figure 111—Status text properties

Status property screen should look similar to the one in Figure 111, *Status text properties*.

Returning to the design screen, you may need to resize and/or reposition the widget margin and the Broadcast Status and Status elements to appear correctly on your display. You can select the magnifying glass icon in the lower left of the design screen to get a sense of the final display size and visual representation of the layout. However, I have found that this can be misleading. Instead, you will more likely have to run the widget, switching back and forth between the runtime version and the design screen to tweak the size and position of the various graphic elements. For my Galaxy Nexus, I settled on the design shown in Figure 112, *Twitch Widget Zoom layout*.

When you are satisfied with the design layout, save the changes by selecting the green check mark icon in the lower-left corner of the screen.

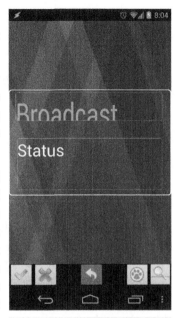

But before we can place the new widget on our home screen and use it, we need to add one more action to our Twitch Channel task. This action will be to tell Tasker which text element to place the results of the %TWITCHRESULT variable into.

Open the Twitch Channel task in Tasker and add the final action. With Zoom installed, you will now see a new Zoom icon and category in the Select Action Category dialog. Select the Zoom category followed by the Zoom Text action. Select the magnifying glass for the Element field. This will pop up a list of Zoom text elements that we created earlier. Choose the "Twitch Channel /Status" element from the list. Then set the Text field to our %TWITCHRESULT variable and save the changes. Once completed, the final Twitch Channel task should look like Figure 113, *Complete Twitch Channel Tasker task*, on page 180.

Figure 112—Twitch Widget Zoom layout

Now that our Twitch Channel task knows where to send its results to be displayed on the widget, we can create the widget by long-pressing the home screen and selecting Widgets. Scroll down to select the Zoom widget. Then choose the Zoom 2x1 option from the list. A pop-up dialog will ask you to select the widget template you want to use. Select the Twitch Channel widget template that we created.

Zoom will then display the Widget Properties dialog as a final design check before placing the widget on the home screen.

But notice that Zoom appended an extra character to the Name property. I'm not sure if this is a bug or a feature, but we need to change the Name field back to the original name by removing whatever character Zoom added to the field. If we don't, the results of the Twitch Channel task won't be able to find our Twitch Channel/Status field. Once the Name property has been corrected, select the green check mark in the lower-left corner to accept the

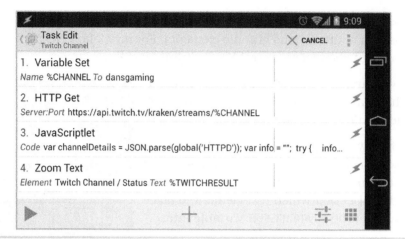

Figure 113—Complete Twitch Channel Tasker task

widget properties. Zoom will then display the design surface to allow you to make any last-minute alterations. Select the green check mark to save the changes and place the widget on your home screen.

Channel Surfing

With the widget on the home screen, we can see whether all our work has been wired up correctly. Select the Broadcast Status text in the widget. What happened? Tasker displayed a brief message on the screen stating External Access Denied - See Prefs/Misc/Allow External Access. That's because Tasker needs to be granted explicit permission to access and control other programs on your Android device, including access to Zoom's widget properties. To grant such permission to Tasker, follow the message's instructions by selecting Preferences from Tasker's main menu. Then select the MISC tab and locate and check the Allow External Access checkbox, as shown in the figure here.

Now that Tasker has been granted external access to programs like Zoom, return to the widget and once again touch the Broadcast Status title text. For example, if you set the %CHANNEL to dansgaming and Dan is broadcasting at the moment, you

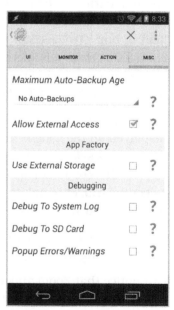

Figure 114—Allowing Tasker external program access

should see the title of Dan's active Twitch broadcast and the number of people currently watching his show.

If Dan isn't currently broadcasting his show or your Android device is not connected to the Internet, the status text will state in red text that his channel is unavailable. When working, your widget may show something similar to Figure 115, *The Custom Twitch.tv Channel Status widget.*

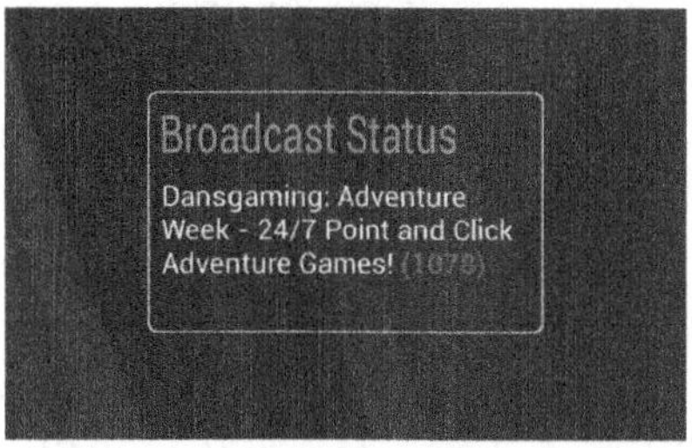

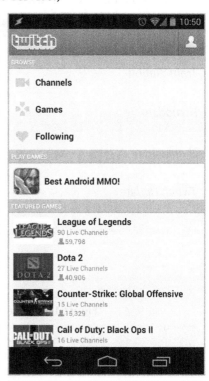

If Dan is broadcasting his show, we can conveniently launch the Twitch client by selecting any part of the status text. (Of course, if you haven't created and/or signed in with a Twitch account already, follow the onscreen prompts to do so. Once you are a registered Twitch.tv member, you can follow other people on the service.)

Figure 115—The Custom Twitch.tv Channel Status widget

If Dan is broadcasting, you can scroll through the channels until you find his username and follow him. Once a username is being followed, it will show up in the Following section of the Twitch Android application, as shown in Figure 116, *The Twitch.tv Android client.*

When I tested my Zoom-based Twitch widget for this book, Dan was broadcasting a week-long twenty-four-hour-a-day adventure-gaming marathon, featuring both live and prerecorded content. So, when I selected his channel from my Following list, a stream of his gaming efforts was played within the Twitch client.

The custom Twitch widget has made monitoring favorite channels so much easier and interactive, and I rarely ever miss a chance to see game players like Dan broadcast live as a result. But even though the option to manually run the Twitch Channel task by touching the Broadcast Status text in the widget is convenient, it would be even more

Figure 116—The Twitch.tv Android client

convenient for Tasker to run the Twitch Channel task at regular intervals. That way, our Twitch widget will work the way most Internet-dependent widgets work on Android, such that it polls for information changes and updates automatically. Let's create a new Tasker profile that automatically runs the Twitch Channel task at regular intervals.

Setting the Update Profile

Launch Tasker and navigate to the PROFILES tab. Create a new profile by selecting the plus icon in the lower toolbar and call the profile Twitch Update. We can choose to run the profile twenty-four hours a day, but because I know I'll be asleep during certain hours and I don't want to unnecessarily run the task, I set my Twitch Update profile to execute from 06:00 (6 a.m.) to 22:00 (10 p.m.). Then I set the profile to run every fifteen minutes. Upon saving the changes, Tasker will ask you to assign a task to the profile. Select the Twitch Channel task. Once configured, the Twitch Update profile should look like the one shown in the following figure.

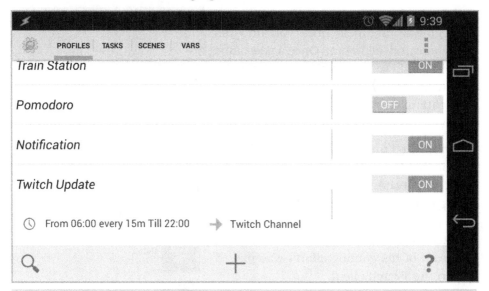

Figure 117—The Twitch Widget Update profile

Now your custom Twitch widget will automatically check every fifteen minutes to see whether users like Dan are actively broadcasting and update the widget's status text accordingly. If you want to query a status update immediately, simply select the Broadcast Status title text on the widget. Monitoring Twitch user broadcast status has never been so easy!

Enhancements

This window into the Twitch.tv web service provides a solid base to further expand upon the possibilities of graphically displaying data from the Internet. It also shows how you can build your own widgets based upon any JSON-conforming web service. You can even combine Tasker scenes with Zoom widgets to create some truly versatile Android programs. Here are a few ideas to keep you Zoom'ing further along:

- Parse an array of usernames to check the broadcast status on more than one user.

- Include additional details from the Twitch.tv JSON data, such as displaying the user icon in the widget.

- Perform a character count on the info variable so you can concatenate the string with ellipses before it exceeds the fixed text area you have defined in your widget.

- Revisit the Forecast.io project and swap out SL4A script with a JavaScriptlet to keep the entire project self-contained within Tasker.

10.3 Next Steps

This concludes our exploration with graphics projects and the book in general. I hope you have enjoyed and learned much throughout this journey. With the knowledge you have gained and the projects that have been completed, you have the ability to quickly create nearly any custom interface or application type that is possible in the standard Android operating system.

While we have done quite a bit with Tasker and SL4A, we have only scratched the surface of what this powerful combination has to offer. Play with the numerous other categories and actions that Tasker exposes. Assemble workflows that do simple tasks and build upon them. If the need arises for more advanced text processing or networking, call upon SL4A to manage that part of the workflow. Depending on the language runtime you configure with SL4A, there are likely thousands of code samples waiting for you on the Web to review and incorporate into your programs.

As you become more comfortable with Tasker and SL4A and want to step up to native Android application development, use the AIDE to codify the workflows you have refined over weeks of iterative testing and tweaking. While the AIDE allows you to quickly change, recompile, and reinstall native Android programs on the device, nothing beats the speed of Tasker and SL4A for on-the-fly task editing and implementation.

Visit the book's online forum to keep the discussion going with me and other Android personalization and automation enthusiasts. Share your experiences, Tasker profiles, tasks, and ideas on what would be some awesome Android workflows. Also take advantage of other communities and documentation on the Web, listed in Appendix 2, *Resources on the Web*, on page 201. They helped me with my own Android projects and will no doubt offer the same level of service for you. Most of all, have fun. Unlike most other mobile operating systems, Android encourages tinkering, tweaking, and out-of-the-box exploration. It was this level of freedom and flexibility that drew me to the Android platform in the first place, and it is bound to only get better with every successive release.

Part IV

Appendixes

Android Programming Tools

One of the advantages that Android's open, true-multitasking platform has over mobile OS competitors such as Apple's iOS is that you can run developer-centric utilities such as AIDE on the device without jailbreaking or rooting the phone or tablet. The open nature attracts tinkerers and developers who want to bring the power of their desktop coding environment onto their post-PC devices. Terminal editors like Nano and Vim can also be used on Android, as well as source version control systems like Git and Subversion. Let's start with a review of some of the best code editors available on Android.

A1.1 Code Editors

Code editors ride waves of popularity depending on the code being written and the target platform that the code will run on. During the early heydays of Unix, Vi and Emacs ruled the roost. Then came GUI desktop environments where rich graphic text editors became the norm. Now that a new platform is emerging, code editors need to evolve to offer a best-in-breed code-authoring experience. However, that will take time to develop as the new way to think about writing code diffuses throughout the phone and tablet coding ecosystem.

Even though Android still has a way to go before its presentation layer matches the rich and creamy user experience on iOS devices, Android benefits from having an active and enthusiastic can-do coding community that often offers up inexpensive or even free solutions to programming needs. Like air, code editors are often taken for granted, but life without them becomes painful rather quickly. Let's take a look at some of the editors that many coders running Android will have a hard time living without.

DroidEdit Pro

If there is one native code editing application that stands out among the rest in the Android app market, it would have to be DroidEdit Pro.[1] Created by André Restivo, DroidEdit Pro offers the most comprehensive language syntax highlighting and secure file copying combination code editor at the time of this writing. The editor supports twenty-five languages, including Assembly, C, C++, C#, Clojure and Scala to Delphi, Pascal and Perl, PHP, Python, and Ruby. Files can be opened from and transferred to DroidEdit Pro via SFTP, Dropbox, and local file system transports. Themes can be customized by color and font size, and the app scales well between phone and tablet screen sizes. An example of what DroidEdit Pro looks like running on an Android phone is shown in the following figure.

DroidEdit Pro is also cloud-friendly in that it can be used to issue remote build commands on the server receiving file transfers like Ruby's Capistrano project. For example, you can create and save a sophisticated build script on the file-receiving server that can be triggered by DroidEdit Pro's Add External Command function. Upon completion of a file transfer, the commands you define are executed on the remote server, and the results of the execution can be displayed in a result screen or in a new or existing document. You can use it to compile C or Java programs and run Ruby or Python scripts or even complex Puppet server workflows.

André offers a free, ad-supported non-Pro version that provides a taste of the full version, but it's not one I would advocate using for the long haul. Besides its lack of remote file transfer support, who wants annoying ads popping in and out while you're trying to concentrate on writing code?

Figure 118—The DroidEdit Pro code editor

- *Pros*: Supports syntax highlighting for many languages, including C/C++, CSS/HTML, Java, JavaScript, Perl, PHP, Python, Ruby, and fifteen others. It can connect directly to Dropbox and OpenSSH/SFTP servers. DroidEdit Pro

---

1. https://play.google.com/store/apps/details?id=com.aor.droidedit.pro

The Best Post-PC Code Editor

With all its useful capabilities, DroidEdit Pro has yet to even come close to the incredible Textastic (http://www.textasticapp.com) which is exclusively available on the iOS platform. For anyone who has used programs like TextMate and Sublime Text 2 on the desktop, Textastic at the time of this writing is the closest you will get to a full-featured editor on any mobile platform. When I checked in with Alexander Blach, Textastic's creator, I never received a reply to my question of Textastic showing up on the Android platform. That leads me to believe it's likely not going to happen any time soon, if ever. While that's a letdown, this leaves a huge opportunity for an enterprising Android developer to take advantage. DroidEdit Pro is a nice start, but it has a long way to go before it comes close to presenting what Textastic has to offer as the gold standard in mobile OS code editing.

can also remotely issue commands to the host server when files are transferred, such as build instructions, workflow direction, and such.

- *Cons*: Cannot extend the editor with plug-ins. You cannot define your own behaviors or syntax highlighting based on file extension. It has harsh default color schemes and an unattractive layout.

- *Price*: $1.91 US.

Terminal IDE

There is one Android Terminal program I consistently use above all others—Terminal IDE.[2] Created by hacker Spartucus Rex, the application's GPLv2-licensed source code and helpful, albeit minimal, documentation are freely available for download from its Google Code project home page.[3]

In addition to providing a clean terminal interface to the rudimentary subset of Linux command-line utilities on Android, Terminal IDE includes an Install System button on its main screen that downloads and installs a vast array of terminal applications. Secure shell, a minimal Java SDK, rsync, git, and many more programs help round out the Terminal IDE experience. And all of this command-line goodness is available for standard devices (no root access required) running Android 2.3 or newer.

One of the neatest things to see Terminal IDE do is run a split-screen tmux session on an Android tablet, as shown in Figure 119, *Terminal IDE running tmux and Vim*, on page 190.

---

2. https://play.google.com/store/apps/details?id=com.spartacusrex.spartacuside
3. http://code.google.com/p/terminal-ide/

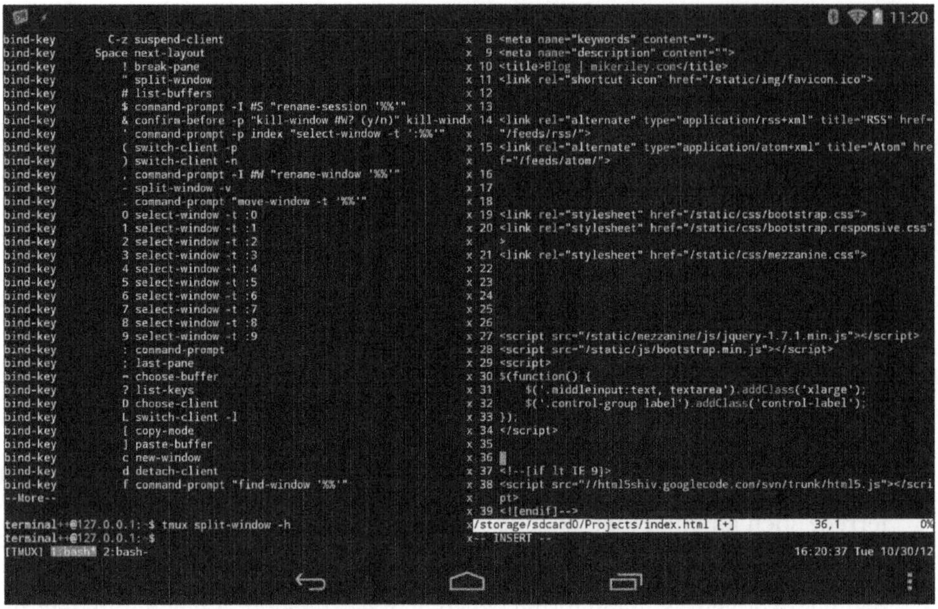

Figure 119—Terminal IDE running tmux and Vim

Try doing that locally on a non-jailbroken iPad! By the way, for those unfamiliar with the joys of using tmux, check out Brian Hogan's *tmux: Productive Mouse-Free Development [Hog12]*. It's an easy read that will make you vastly more productive when operating within a terminal window.

Of course, the point of including Terminal IDE in the category of code editors is because the system install includes one of my favorite terminal-based code editors, Vim. (Incidentally, fellow Pragmatic Bookshelf author Drew Neil's *Practical Vim: Edit Text at the Speed of Thought [Nei12]* is an excellent book to refer to if you're learning Vim.) Terminal IDE's version of Vim already has a number of Vim extensions preconfigured for HTML and Java development. Autocomplete, tag lookup, navigational key mapping, and more make you immediately productive without having to start Vim with the usual bare-bones minimum features. If you are a power Vim user with a favorite .vimrc file, just copy it to the /data/data/com.spatacusrex.spartacuside/files path that serves as your home directory, and Vim will behave exactly as you would expect.

You can even build Android .apk files using the Java kit installed by Terminal IDE, though I still find working within AIDE, even with its less-than-Vim GUI-based editor, easier thanks to the visual interface it provides. Still, it's nice to know that if you don't want to spend the money for a fully operational AIDE license, Terminal IDE provides all the tools you need to replicate the compiled native Android application outcome.

One last killer feature available as a result of Terminal IDE's system install is the inclusion of Telnet and SSH daemons that you can run on your Android. Doing so allows you to SSH into your Android device from another computer on your network, all without having to even root your phone or tablet to do so. Wireless file copying and editing on the device is not only possible, it's downright cool.

Terminal IDE runs on both Android phones and tablets, but as you can imagine, the small screen on the phone makes a multipaned terminal session (pardon the pun) multipained. Unless you have the eyesight of a hawk and the patience of a saint, editing anything more than a simple script file in Terminal IDE on a phone is a hassle. But given the much more expansive screen real estate on a tablet, Terminal IDE is an ideal utility to have at the ready. The app also includes an onscreen keyboard replacement that can be swapped out via the Language & input panel within the Android Settings application. The keyboard adds much-needed terminal keys that are not included with the standard Android onscreen keyboard, such as the Escape, function, special character, and arrow keys. Considering all that is bundled with Terminal IDE, it's a shining example of the open source ideology on the Android platform.

- *Pros*: Comprehensive terminal package with a slew of useful, preconfigured command-line utilities. It does not require root-level access to install and use. It includes useful onscreen keyboard replacement optimized to work with terminal entry. It's also free with source code available for download and study.

- *Cons*: Some lesser used but useful command-line apps like Subversion are not included. It has limited Java implementation. When using most terminal applications, especially Vim and tmux, it requires a Bluetooth keyboard to be useful and effective.

- *Price*: Free.

Emacs

For every Vi/Vim fan, there is an Emacs fan. Android coders are no exception, which is why developer zielmicha ported GNU Emacs to the Android platform.[4] The 1.33MB installer available in the Play Store requires an additional 22MB

---

4. https://play.google.com/store/apps/details?id=com.zielm.emacs

download from the http://emacs.zielm.com website to run the included busyboxrc.sh.dl bash shell script. This in turn downloads, decompresses, and installs the terminfo.tar.lzma, etc.tar.lzma, lisp.tar.lzma, and emacs.bin.lzma library dependencies. After everything is set up and running, the editor delivers all the power that the desktop version of Emacs has to offer on mobile devices.

An editor like Emacs that was initially designed for a desktop-centric experience practically requires a Bluetooth keyboard (though you could also install Klaus Weidner's popular Hacker's Keyboard onscreen keyboard replacement if necessary[5]) and large tablet screen to work effectively on Android. Yet for those with Emacs keystrokes embedded into their muscle memory, Emacs for Android has arrived. See the following figure.

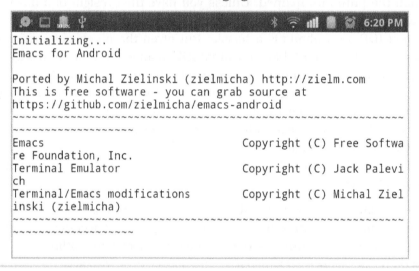

Figure 120—The full Emacs experience on Android

- *Pros*: Full Emacs implementation on Android. It is fully compatible with desktop .emacs configuration files. And like most good open source projects, the app is free with the GPL source code available for download.

- *Cons*: Large install with large memory footprint for just one application (albeit a powerful one). It really requires an Android tablet and Bluetooth keyboard to do anything useful with the editor. It might not run on all Android devices.

- *Price*: Free.

---

5.   https://play.google.com/store/apps/details?id=org.pocketworkstation.pckeyboard

TextWarrior

While not optimized as a code editor per se, TextWarrior by MyopicMobile is a text editor that nevertheless has basic syntax support for several languages, including C, C++, Objective-C, C#, Java, JavaScript, PHP, Python, and Ruby.[6] It's also a native Android application, with its own unique spin on the usual Android user interface in order to better facilitate the text-editing experience on a small touchscreen. Perhaps the best feature that TextWarrior has above less industrial-strength editors is its ability to load large files, as shown in the following figure.

TextWarrior also features a text clipboard on a virtual shelf that slides in and out of the screen, as well as the usual auto-indent and word wrapping that is expected with modern-day editors. Word and character count are also standard, as is its unique ability to copy selected text dragged onto a target area. All this, combined with the free open source software license, makes TextWarrior a text editor worth installing.

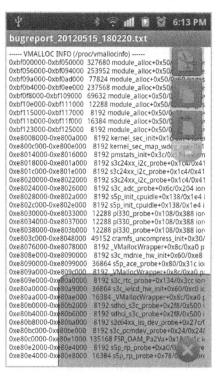

Figure 121—Viewing a large debug file using TextWarrior

- *Pros*: Handles large text files that would crash other GUI-based Android text editors. It has a drag-and-drop text editing interface. It supports a rudimentary set of markup and programming languages, and it's free.

- *Cons*: Does not syntax highlight HTML or XML. It can have problems with nonstandard Android onscreen keyboards. The interface and cursor operation take time to get used to.

- *Price*: Free.

A1.2 Source Version Control

I have worked with a number of open source and proprietary source version control systems. When Subversion (SVN) arrived in the year 2000, it forced

---

6.   https://play.google.com/store/apps/details?id=com.myopicmobile.textwarrior.android

people to recalibrate how source control should work in a broadly defined network. It also fixed a number of shortcomings and issues compared to existing version control systems, one of the more popular being the original Unix-centric Concurrent Versions System (CVS), at the time the most prevalent source management system available.

However, SVN was eclipsed by Git, a distributed version control system (DVCS). Git combines the best of what both CVS and SVN had to offer by allowing developers to work and manage source code in an entirely distributed and disconnected way. Unlike SVN, which requires online connectivity to the central server when committing changes to the source code repository, Git allows for local commits, branches, and merges to happen entirely on the developer's computer. The developer's computer can also serve as the source code client or server, and a network connection to a centralized source is required only when developers need to "push" their changes to that location. Let's take a look at some of the source control options available on the Android platform.

Git

Git is bundled in two products we have already evaluated: AIDE and Terminal IDE. AIDE's version of Git is unlocked when the AIDE Premium key is purchased. Terminal IDE is included for free as part of the system installation option. Both offer full Git pull/merge/commit/push functionality that you can perform from desktop versions of the source control utility. However, neither offers a graphical interface showing diffs across commits. For that, Android developer Roberto Tyler has created a read-only paid Git client called Agit.[7] When this application is combined with either AIDE's or Terminal IDE's version of Git, you will have the full Git desktop experience on your Android device, as shown in Figure 122, *Running Git via Terminal IDE*, on page 195.

If you're already an experienced Git user, the Terminal IDE version works exactly as you would expect. In addition to managing code, you could use this onboard version management system for more than just code. Combine it with Vim's Git extensions (vim-fugitive is awesome,[8] though git.vim will do the job as well[9]), and you can version manage just about anything you create. You could host your own internal Git server to sync and back up all your work, or you can rely on external providers such as GitHub to manage the backend for you.

---

7.   https://play.google.com/store/apps/details?id=com.madgag.agit
8.   https://github.com/tpope/vim-fugitive
9.   https://github.com/motemen/git-vim

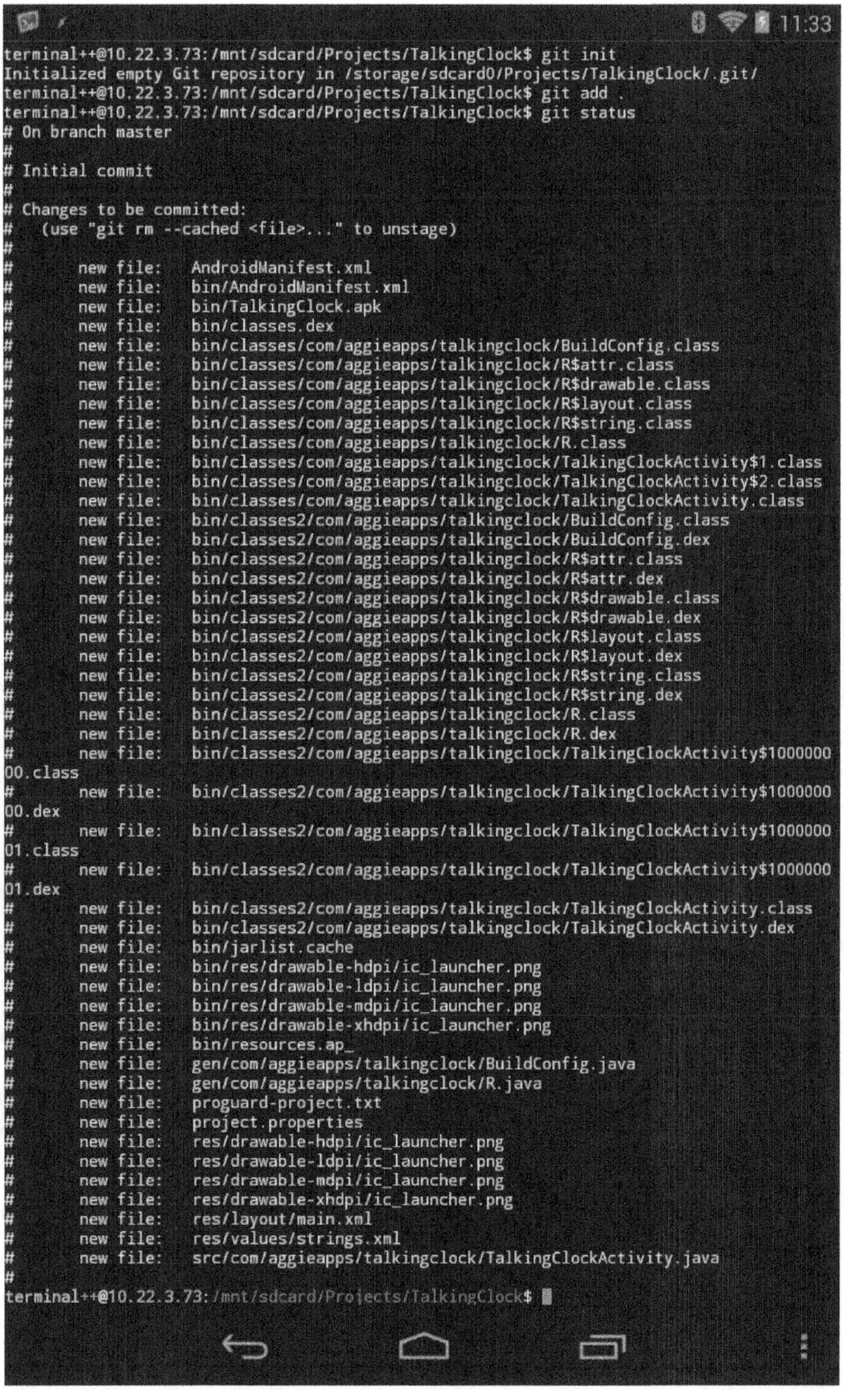

Figure 122—Running Git via Terminal IDE

If you're not already familiar with Git and would like to learn how to use it and quickly understand why it has taken the developer world by storm, check out Travis Swicegood's book *Pragmatic Guide to Git [Swi10]*, published by Pragmatic Bookshelf.

- *Pros*: Free. It has exceptional DCVS.

- *Cons*: No GUI-friendly read-write Git client exists yet on Android, although developer Roberto Tyler aspires that his Agit client will achieve this status one day, eventually. However, I have been waiting for nearly a year to see this much-needed functionality added, so I have low expectations that Agit will receive such an upgrade any time soon.

- *Price*: Free.

Mercurial

Even though Mercurial never really gained the kind of sizable following that Subversion and Git achieved, it is an excellent DVCS still in use. It is especially popular among die-hard Python coders. Android developer Spencer Elliot created one of the first of the few Mercurial clients available as a free download from the Google Play store. Mercury,[10] shown in the figure here, is a well-intentioned Mercurial client that works from a rudimentary level but falls short on execution. Given that the application hasn't been updated in more than two years, it may eventually dissipate into the ether along with Mercurial.

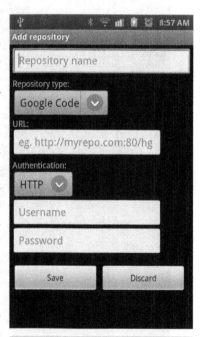

Figure 123—Mercury for Android

- *Pros*: One of the only Mercurial-compatible clients available on Google Play. It can import Mercurial repositories from popular public Mercurial repositories such as Google Code, Bitbucket, and CodePlex. It's free.

- *Cons*: Read-only client with bare-bones beta interface. It does not support secure repositories, and it's yet another application that unnecessarily requires it automatically start at boot time.

- *Price*: Free.

---

10. https://play.google.com/store/apps/details?id=ca.spencerelliott.mercury

Subversion

Even though these days Subversion has taken a backseat to Git, there is still a mountain of legacy projects and workflow systems built around SVN that will be in place for a long time to come. And now that the Apache Project manages the Subversion codebase, its pedigree has been solidified into the pantheon of great (for its time) software upon which even better software (like Git) can rest upon its giant shoulders.

While several Subversion clients are available for Android, I prefer the paid OASVN PRO.[11] OASVN delivers the full Subversion experience in a native Android GUI application. While I do wish Terminal IDE had an SVN installation option, OASVN is a working alternative. However, OASVN does not have the most attractive interface, as you can see in the following figure.

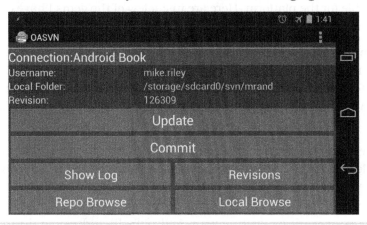

Figure 124—Open Android SVN PRO (OASVN)

It is also slow compared to the desktop version of Subversion. Even small, single-character changes can take minutes (or longer, depending on the number of source files being managed) to synchronize with an SVN server. But it's one of the only Subversion clients available in the Google Play store that offers full read-write checkout, updates, commits, and reverts. OASVN also supports file conflict resolution as well as local and remote file repository browsing. Until an Android terminal-based Subversion client is available, OASVN PRO is the best option Subversion users have to date on the Android platform.

---

11. https://play.google.com/store/apps/details?id=com.valleytg.oasvn.android

To learn more about Subversion, read Mike Mason's book titled *Pragmatic Version Control Using Subversion [Mas06]*, also published by Pragmatic Bookshelf.

- *Pros*: Stable and actively maintained. The Pro version supports full SVN updates and commits.

- *Cons*: Kludgey interface. It's slow. There is no GUI-based diff visualization.

- *Price*: Free.

A1.3 Miscellaneous Tools

Given how developer- and hacker-friendly the Android OS is, it should come as no surprise that a vast array of free and paid developer-centric utilities are available for the platform. Here are just a few of the gems I have discovered in my own Android application explorations.

AndroZip File Manager[12] is a feature-complete file archiver application for Android that supports a variety of compressed file types, including GZIP, RAR, TAR, and ZIP. This program really comes in handy when zipping up a project to send as an email file attachment or post for download from a website link.

PHP developers will appreciate the free LAMP-like stack for Android by DK Labs called KSWEB.[13] Not only will you be able to write your PHP code using the text editors discussed earlier, but with KSWEB, you will also be able to locally test and debug your PHP code. You can even have others view the results of your work by visiting your Android's IP address and project URL with a web browser.

Need to move files on and off your Android device via standard FTP? FTP Server,[14] a fork from the original (but now dead) SwiFTP FTP Server, delivers a basic and intuitive FTP server on Android.

Nic Raboy's SQLTool Pro Database Editor is an inexpensive app that can be used to directly connect to and edit MySQL, Oracle PostgreSQL, and SQL Server databases.[15] Query results can be exported to CSV. It works best on tablets.

---

12. https://play.google.com/store/apps/details?id=com.agilesoftresource
13. https://play.google.com/store/apps/details?id=ru.kslabs.ksweb
14. https://play.google.com/store/apps/details?id=be.ppareit.swiftp
15. https://play.google.com/store/apps/details?id=com.nraboy.sqltool

If you're a developer who prefers using the Git and Mercurial-supported Bit-bucket DVCS service,[16] Saibotd's free and open sourced application called Bitbeaker offers a clean, Android-friendly interface to this GitHub competitor.[17]

For those looking to reminisce with ancient DOS-based coding tools and utilities like Turbo Pascal and VisiCalc,[18] check out AnDOSBox,[19] one of the better DOS emulators available on Android.

Hundreds of other excellent code-centric utilities are available for download from the Google Play store. Google has made searching for applications a breeze via the Play Store Android app or the Play Store website.[20] You will likely find what you are looking for.

16. http://www.bitbucket.org
17. https://play.google.com/store/apps/details?id=ca.spencerelliott.mercury
18. http://edn.embarcadero.com/article/20803 and http://www.bricklin.com/history/vcexecutable.htm, respec-tively.
19. https://play.google.com/store/apps/details?id=com.locnet.dosbox
20. https://play.google.com/store/apps

Resources on the Web

Here is a list of helpful links to articles, forums, and other information available on the Internet to further your learning of Android automation, customization, and programming:

- Android AIDE on Google+ is the community forum where the developers of AIDE interact with users, post links to the latest AIDE-related articles, and offer insights on how to get the most out of programming Android with the AIDE.[1]

- Android Scripting Tutorials is a listing maintained on the SL4A Google Code–hosted website that features links to dozens of articles and projects highlighting SL4A in action.[2]

- Pocketables Tasker Articles is a variety of Tasker-related articles ranging from a detailed walk-through of the product to a series of how-to articles to implement or gain additional inspiration for your own projects.[3]

- Reddit Tasker Forum is a popular location on the Web where both amateur and experienced Tasker users go to ask questions, post helpful and unique Tasker applications, and engage with fellow fans of the program.[4]

- Stack Overflow SL4A Tagged Questions offers a developer-to-developer ranked question and answer forum for people seeking assistance with SL4A-hosted scripts.[5]

---

1. https://plus.google.com/101304250883271700981/posts
2. http://code.google.com/p/android-scripting/wiki/Tutorials
3. http://www.pocketables.com/2013/03/overview-of-pocketables-tasker-articles.html
4. http://www.reddit.com/r/Tasker
5. http://stackoverflow.com/questions/tagged/sl4a

- Tasker Wiki is a comprehensive resource guide for Tasker that features links to the Tasker online user guide, along with a number of custom Tasker profile, scene, and task walk-throughs and links to third-party Tasker plug-ins and supported tools.[6]

---

6.   http://tasker.wikidot.com

Bibliography

[Bur10]   Ed Burnette. *Hello, Android: Introducing Google's Mobile Development Platform*. The Pragmatic Bookshelf, Raleigh, NC and Dallas, TX, Third Edition, 2010.

[CGMW13] Jennifer Campbell, Paul Gries, Jason Montojo, and Greg Wilson. *Practical Programming: An Introduction to Computer Science Using Python 3*. The Pragmatic Bookshelf, Raleigh, NC and Dallas, TX, Second Edition, 2013.

[Fri97]   Jeffrey E. F. Friedl. *Mastering Regular Expressions*. O'Reilly & Associates, Inc., Sebastopol, CA, 1997.

[Hog12]   Brian P. Hogan. *tmux: Productive Mouse-Free Development*. The Pragmatic Bookshelf, Raleigh, NC and Dallas, TX, 2012.

[Mas06]   Mike Mason. *Pragmatic Version Control Using Subversion*. The Pragmatic Bookshelf, Raleigh, NC and Dallas, TX, 2006.

[Nei12]   Drew Neil. *Practical Vim: Edit Text at the Speed of Thought*. The Pragmatic Bookshelf, Raleigh, NC and Dallas, TX, 2012.

[Nö09]   Staffan Nöteberg. *Pomodoro Technique Illustrated: The Easy Way to Do More in Less Time*. The Pragmatic Bookshelf, Raleigh, NC and Dallas, TX, 2009.

[Pin09]   Chris Pine. *Learn to Program*. The Pragmatic Bookshelf, Raleigh, NC and Dallas, TX, Second Edition, 2009.

[Ril12]   Mike Riley. *Programming Your Home*. The Pragmatic Bookshelf, Raleigh, NC and Dallas, TX, 2012.

[Sau12]   Daniel Sauter. *Rapid Android Development: Build Rich, Sensor-Based Applications with Processing*. The Pragmatic Bookshelf, Raleigh, NC and Dallas, TX, 2012.

[Swi10]   Travis Swicegood. *Pragmatic Guide to Git*. The Pragmatic Bookshelf, Raleigh, NC and Dallas, TX, 2010.

[TFH13]   David Thomas, Chad Fowler, and Andrew Hunt. *Programming Ruby 1.9 & 2.0: The Pragmatic Programmer's Guide*. The Pragmatic Bookshelf, Raleigh, NC and Dallas, TX, Fourth Edition, 2013.

Index

Android Apps and 3D for Kids

Create mobile apps for Android phones and tablets, and get your kids (ages 10-99) writing 3D games in JavaScript.

Create mobile apps for Android phones and tablets faster and more easily than you ever imagined. Use "Processing," the free, award-winning, graphics-savvy language and development environment, to work with the touchscreens, hardware sensors, cameras, network transceivers, and other devices and software in the latest Android phones and tablets.

Daniel Sauter
(392 pages) ISBN: 9781937785062. $33
http://pragprog.com/book/dsproc

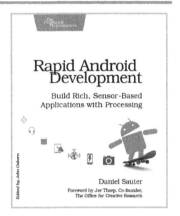

You know what's even better than playing games? Creating your own. Even if you're an absolute beginner, this book will teach you how to make your own online games with interactive examples. You'll learn programming using nothing more than a browser, and see cool, 3D results as you type. You'll learn real-world programming skills in a real programming language: Java-Script, the language of the web. You'll be amazed at what you can do as you build interactive worlds and fun games. Appropriate for ages 10-99!

Chris Strom
(250 pages) ISBN: 9781937785444. $36
http://pragprog.com/book/csjava

Long Live the Command Line!

Use tmux and Vim for incredible mouse-free productivity.

Your mouse is slowing you down. The time you spend context switching between your editor and your consoles eats away at your productivity. Take control of your environment with tmux, a terminal multiplexer that you can tailor to your workflow. Learn how to customize, script, and leverage tmux's unique abilities and keep your fingers on your keyboard's home row.

Brian P. Hogan
(88 pages) ISBN: 9781934356968. $16.25
http://pragprog.com/book/bhtmux

Vim is a fast and efficient text editor that will make you a faster and more efficient developer. It's available on almost every OS—if you master the techniques in this book, you'll never need another text editor. In more than 100 Vim tips, you'll quickly learn the editor's core functionality and tackle your trickiest editing and writing tasks.

Drew Neil
(346 pages) ISBN: 9781934356982. $29
http://pragprog.com/book/dnvim

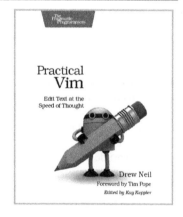

Android Apps and 3D for Kids

Create mobile apps for Android phones and tablets, and get your kids (ages 10-99) writing 3D games in JavaScript.

Create mobile apps for Android phones and tablets faster and more easily than you ever imagined. Use "Processing," the free, award-winning, graphics-savvy language and development environment, to work with the touchscreens, hardware sensors, cameras, network transceivers, and other devices and software in the latest Android phones and tablets.

Daniel Sauter
(392 pages) ISBN: 9781937785062. $33
http://pragprog.com/book/dsproc

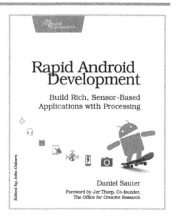

You know what's even better than playing games? Creating your own. Even if you're an absolute beginner, this book will teach you how to make your own online games with interactive examples. You'll learn programming using nothing more than a browser, and see cool, 3D results as you type. You'll learn real-world programming skills in a real programming language: JavaScript, the language of the web. You'll be amazed at what you can do as you build interactive worlds and fun games. Appropriate for ages 10-99!

Chris Strom
(250 pages) ISBN: 9781937785444. $36
http://pragprog.com/book/csjava

Long Live the Command Line!

Use tmux and Vim for incredible mouse-free productivity.

Your mouse is slowing you down. The time you spend context switching between your editor and your consoles eats away at your productivity. Take control of your environment with tmux, a terminal multiplexer that you can tailor to your workflow. Learn how to customize, script, and leverage tmux's unique abilities and keep your fingers on your keyboard's home row.

Brian P. Hogan
(88 pages) ISBN: 9781934356968. $16.25
http://pragprog.com/book/bhtmux

Vim is a fast and efficient text editor that will make you a faster and more efficient developer. It's available on almost every OS—if you master the techniques in this book, you'll never need another text editor. In more than 100 Vim tips, you'll quickly learn the editor's core functionality and tackle your trickiest editing and writing tasks.

Drew Neil
(346 pages) ISBN: 9781934356982. $29
http://pragprog.com/book/dnvim

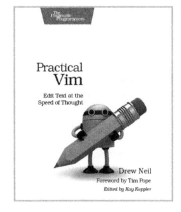

Seven in Seven

Go beyond learning a new language—learn seven. And get up to speed on the latest NoSQL databases.

You should learn a programming language every year, as recommended by *The Pragmatic Programmer*. But if one per year is good, how about *Seven Languages in Seven Weeks*? In this book you'll get a hands-on tour of Clojure, Haskell, Io, Prolog, Scala, Erlang, and Ruby. Whether or not your favorite language is on that list, you'll broaden your perspective of programming by examining these languages side-by-side. You'll learn something new from each, and best of all, you'll learn how to learn a language quickly.

Bruce A. Tate
(330 pages) ISBN: 9781934356593. $34.95
http://pragprog.com/book/btlang

Data is getting bigger and more complex by the day, and so are your choices in handling it. From traditional RDBMS to newer NoSQL approaches, *Seven Databases in Seven Weeks* takes you on a tour of some of the hottest open source databases today. In the tradition of Bruce A. Tate's *Seven Languages in Seven Weeks*, this book goes beyond your basic tutorial to explore the essential concepts at the core of each technology.

Eric Redmond and Jim R. Wilson
(354 pages) ISBN: 9781934356920. $35
http://pragprog.com/book/rwdata

The Pragmatic Bookshelf

The Pragmatic Bookshelf features books written by developers for developers. The titles continue the well-known Pragmatic Programmer style and continue to garner awards and rave reviews. As development gets more and more difficult, the Pragmatic Programmers will be there with more titles and products to help you stay on top of your game.

Visit Us Online

This Book's Home Page
http://pragprog.com/book/mrand
Source code from this book, errata, and other resources. Come give us feedback, too!

Register for Updates
http://pragprog.com/updates
Be notified when updates and new books become available.

Join the Community
http://pragprog.com/community
Read our weblogs, join our online discussions, participate in our mailing list, interact with our wiki, and benefit from the experience of other Pragmatic Programmers.

New and Noteworthy
http://pragprog.com/news
Check out the latest pragmatic developments, new titles and other offerings.

Save on the eBook

Save on the eBook versions of this title. Owning the paper version of this book entitles you to purchase the electronic versions at a terrific discount.

PDFs are great for carrying around on your laptop—they are hyperlinked, have color, and are fully searchable. Most titles are also available for the iPhone and iPod touch, Amazon Kindle, and other popular e-book readers.

Buy now at *http://pragprog.com/coupon*

Contact Us

Online Orders:	*http://pragprog.com/catalog*
Customer Service:	*support@pragprog.com*
International Rights:	*translations@pragprog.com*
Academic Use:	*academic@pragprog.com*
Write for Us:	*http://pragprog.com/write-for-us*
Or Call:	+1 800-699-7764

CPSIA information can be obtained at www.ICGtesting.com
Printed in the USA
LVOW02s1752121113

361024LV00011BA/26/P